COWGIRL LOGIC

Short stories containing wisdom to live by
(With a sprinkling of stupidity mixed
in just for entertainment's sake)

BY
CRYSTAL LYONS

STRATTON
-PRESS-
Publishing Life

COWGIRL LOGIC
Copyright © 2020 **Crystal Lyons**

Stratton Press Publishing
831 N Tatnall Street Suite M #188,
Wilmington, DE 19801
www.stratton-press.com
1-888-323-7009

Because of the dynamic nature of the Internet, any web addresses or links contained in this book may have changed since publication and may no longer be valid. The views expressed in the work are solely those of the author and do not necessarily reflect the views of the publisher, and the publisher hereby disclaims any responsibility for them.

ISBN (Paperback): 978-1-64345-658-4
ISBN (Ebook): 978-1-64345-880-9

Printed in the United States of America

Contents

ACKNOWLEDGMENTS

I want to dedicate this book to all my incredibly wonderful and crazy friends who I've been blessed to know along the way as I've lived my life among country folk and rodeo contestants. There are obviously too many to mention. My mom and dad, Paul and Juanita Mangold, who instilled in me the courage to follow my heart. My two amazing sons, Tyger Tuff and Colt Wrangler, through whom God has richly blessed my life. Jesus, my Redeemer, You're awesome! Holy Spirit, my strengthener, You're brilliant! Abba Father, my inheritance, You're amazing! And the three are actually ONE…wrap your brain around that!

INTRODUCTION

God speaks. As I once heard someone say, God didn't write a book and then lose His voice! He speaks in a variety of ways, and in our journey through life, it behooves us to become acquainted with the many ways that He communicates. He obviously speaks to me through His written Word, but He also speaks through dreams and visions, as well as that quiet whisper down on the inside, or simply a "knowing" that is easier to recognize than it is to explain. But also, one of the ways He communicates to me is through life's interactions with animals; oh, how He uses animals to communicate a truth to me!

Relationships are made and strengthened through accurate communication, or lost through a lack thereof. It's no different with God. You can't know Him without being relational, and you can't develop a healthy relationship without communication. Communication is not a one-way street. Knowing His heart can't truly be accomplished without hearing His voice and learning His ways. It is my desire that this book not only carry with it profound truths made simple, but at the same time, bring encouragement and correction if necessary. But knowledge about something is often boring, in contrast to experiencing it! My desire is to stir a greater hunger in each reader, to know the Father's heart and recognize His voice, which always leads to experiencing Him! Let the adventures begin!

Words Release Actions

I remember the day we bought him. He was really little, kinda ugly, but full of passion. We were living in the Ozarks at the time, and we had started catching wild cattle. His name was J.J. He was a pit bull pup, not much older than twelve weeks, but he was already catching small pigs for training. We bought him and brought him home.

My dad had a big laugh. "You're going to do what with this mutt?" My dad had coonhounds, and this little guy looked...well...small and helpless.

Every morning at daylight, Dad would go out to milk the cow. Sometimes she would come to the barn on her own, and sometimes she wouldn't (we could always tell by distant sounds of cussing). J.J. was always looking to go with "whomever" to do "whatever," and Dad got into the habit of "siccing" J.J. on the cow. Of course, J.J. was too little to even see over the tall grass, but his ears would go up in excitement, and Dad would just belly laugh. We kept telling Dad he was gonna be sorry one day for saying that. He'd just laugh. Until...

One morning, the cow wasn't going in. Dad was cussing the cow and hissing at J.J. I guess Dad hadn't noticed how the little guy had grown. Suddenly J.J. caught sight of "ole Betsy," and it was "Katie bar the door!"

J.J. couldn't quite catch her totally, but he got close enough to grab hold of her bag. Dad's cussing was more "passionate," the cow was bawling, and J.J. was hanging tight! We ran outside in time to see the cow running hard and fast toward the barn with a small black object hanging down between her back legs.

Well, we finally pried J.J. off the cow's bag and got her settled down to normal...along with Dad's blood pressure. The cow had an extra big bag for a week or two, but it eventually healed up and she was good as new. Dad never hissed at J.J. again unless he wanted what he said.

Words are like that. They may seem small and insignificant, but they are powerful and they bring about events...either for good or for evil. God's Word says in the book of James chapter 3 that our tongue is like the rudder of a ship. It may be small, but it controls the direction. Proverbs 18:21 says, "Death and life are in the power of the tongue, and those who love it will eat the fruit thereof." We can be just like my dad, releasing words and not even realizing their impact. Words like, "Nothing ever works out for me" or "No matter how much money we have, it's never enough" or "If it weren't for bad luck, I'd have no luck at all." Then they laugh, just like my dad…not knowing the "wrecks" they are releasing in their lives. If we KNEW that whatever came out of our mouth would instantly come to pass, we would talk totally different than we do. Statements like, "I'm sick and tired of…" or "I about died!" would be stricken from our vocabulary.

Oh well, one good thing DID come out of it. From that day forward, all Dad had to do was take Mom's little froufrou house dog out with him, and the cow would hit a trot to the barn.

Having a little fun on my super cool stallion!

Snake Tales

Few things scare me more than snakes. I remember once, while playing in a creek, I looked down in time to see a snake swim between my legs. I came close to walking on water that day and skinned up both my shins trying to climb up the creek bank; my mother, instead of coming to my aid, was beating the ground, laughing hilariously. Like she often said, "Snakes don't endanger us near as much as we endanger ourselves by our own panic."

Living next to a river in the Ozarks, snakes were just a part of life. They were in the chicken house, under the house, in the barn, in the river, and in the hay fields. Nothing can make you wet your pants any quicker than grabbing up a bale of hay and a snake's head is sticking out! I hate that. But more than anything, I hate a snake in the house.

One time while walking by the bathroom, I heard something and looked just in time to see a huge chicken snake fall off the log wall and into the tub. It was a definite, sickening kind of "thud" sound that sent uncontrollable shivers up my spine and an uncontrollable scream out my mouth. Then in horror, I watched as its head moved around the top rim of the tub. The "screaming shivers" took over, and I totally lost control. The snake went "somewhere"…that was the problem. I never took a relaxing bath in that tub after that.

About a month later, I was on the phone and noticed my cat intently looking at something. I stuck my head around the corner to see what was holding the cat's attention. It was that big chicken snake crawling through the kitchen. Determined not to let him get away this time, I threw down the phone, grabbed the .22 pistol, and began shooting. As the snake was crawling from room to room, I would scream, jump up on top of furniture, and fire more rounds. It never dawned on me what this was doing to the person on the other end of the phone! Or my house. My friend didn't know whether to call the police or keep listening! She said one second she was talking, and the next, I threw the phone down and screamed, "He's back!" After that, all she heard was lots of commotion with intermittent screams and gunshots! Poor lady! I could have given her a heart attack. I emptied the gun before thinking about my friend on the phone. When it all settled down, we had a good laugh out of it. Everybody in that neck of the woods heard about it, making comments like, "Heard you shot up your house!"

It was Franklin D. Roosevelt who said, "All we have to fear is fear itself." He was right, you know. The fact THAT we fear is more harmful to us than WHAT we fear! Well, after it was all over; I survived, my neighbor survived…the snake survived also.

All-Girl Rodeo Hereford, TX 1986

What Kind of Earplugs Do You Have?

Our youngest son, Colt Wrangler, had shot his first buck—a nice eight-pointer; got him with one shot through the heart at around 225 yards. He was excited, and so were we. Our friend who took him hunting got it all on video. It's cute.

After the shot was made and they're all still whispering (you know, like they do on those hunting shows you men watch on TV), he brings the video camera slowly back to Colt. There was Colt with his special "earplugs" stuck in his ears, grinning like a traveling rat. He shoots with empty .223 casings stuck in each ear. It looks like something out of Frankenstein. Colt swears it works great. While our friend is trying to control his laughter and still "narrate" this fine piece of video work, he says that they've found that the empty gun casings kinda work as a "buck fever absorber," enabling the hunter to make steadier shots. We may need to patent the idea.

I'm figuring out that we've all got areas in our life where we wear self-styled earplugs. I got 'em. You probably do, too. Though mine may be different than yours, the purpose is still the same. I wear 'em so I don't hear things that make me uncomfortable. Like, I won't listen to my own music CDs. I avoid having to listen to myself at all costs. You may think that's being humble, but trust me, it's not. If anything, it's just the opposite. I don't like to listen because I will then have to face my own imperfections and inabilities. It's easier to deceive myself this way. If I can just avoid listening, then I don't have to face some things that need to be changed and improved. But when it's time to go back into the studio to record a new project, it's especially tough 'cause you gotta face who you are. Those microphones don't lie (I hate that). As long as I can avoid it, I can convince myself I can sing as good as any of my favorite singers. But when I actually face the truth, I am only me, for whatever that's worth. But is that so bad? I mean, the sooner I can stop comparing myself to something I can never be, the sooner I can face the truth of who I am. When I feel like I can face the truth, I have courage to remove the earplugs! Once I remove the earplugs, I can start working on things that need to be improved.

What do your "earplugs" look like? What is it you don't want to face? A bad marriage relationship? A life that didn't turn out the way you planned? Still comparing yourself to something you were never meant to be? If we can just begin to realize the value of our lives, other people, and what we have in life, we can start taking out the "earplugs" and begin to listen, really listen. We might hear some things we don't like hearing and don't want to face, but only in "hearing" can we fix what could never be fixed while we go through life with our earplugs in! Life is too short to protect ourselves from the truth.

Well, I've told you a little about one set of earplugs that I have. I figure I probably have some other sets fitted for other areas, but hey, let's just work on one area at a time. How 'bout you? What do your "earplugs" look like?

REMOVING THE THORN

Ever get a thorn or sticker in you that you can't see, but oh, when something touches that area, you sure KNOW it's there! Well, just like we can get that in the physical, we can have them in our mind and emotions. A while back, I slowly became aware of a thought process that I had every time I would notice a man of honor who had accomplished things in his life. The thoughts that were always connected to recognizing a man of such qualities were, "A man like that would never even notice someone like me." I suddenly realized I had a problem. WHY do I always think like that? Where did that come from?

Knowing that we simply cannot rise above our thoughts, I wanted this inner belief system out of my thinking! Our own screwed up mind-sets will sabotage our future if we allow them to remain. So I asked the Lord to reveal to me WHERE I got this attitude. The answer came rather quickly. I was suddenly back…way back…remembering a very painful scene. Most people don't know this, but I was married once, fresh out of high school, before I married the father of my two wonderful sons. He was a hometown boy I had always admired…handsome, athletic, and talented in so many ways, one of those rare guys who can do just about anything he sets his mind to. I was THRILLED when he looked my way. But about five years into the marriage, he discovered that my father was handing down the family farm to my brother and not to me. It was a wonderful 320 acres, backed up to National Forest, with a river running through the length of it, six springs, and one artesian well. Quite the rare piece of real estate! It eventually came out rather cruelly that he never desired me, but had only wanted the farm. BINGO! There it is! That hidden thorn that you can't see in all the confidence exuded in the personality of a person…until something touches it. There it was, the origin of a belief system that would hold me to a lower standard of living if not removed. I allowed my first husband to put such a low value on me…and worse, I unknowingly accepted his value system as accurate!

We CANNOT rise above the legal contracts we have made agreements with. Those contracts must be destroyed, and WE must come out of agreement with them to break their power over our lives. I repented for agreeing with a value of myself set by another and not the value that my Father places on me. We tend to align ourselves with those moments that come with strong emotions. That's why truths created during trauma can have a stronger hold on us than the higher truth from God's Word. I forgave the individual connected to this memory—just in case I needed to do so—even though I have felt no animosity toward him for years.

I can't say that my whole thinking process has immediately changed. I have to consciously guard against those negative thoughts and replace them with truth. But at least the "thorn" has been discovered and removed! What agreements have you made as a result of past traumatic events that are now ruling over you? Have you agreed with a mind-set that's based on fear? Or hate? Or deep emotional trauma? Ask the Lord to show you where the source of those thoughts are based, and hold on tight because He's liable to take you back in time so that thorn can be found…and removed!

A Bitter Pill to Swallow

During the time that I was riding rough stock, I once entered a little "Po-dunk" all-girl rodeo in Arkansas. I hadn't been riding bulls that long, but I'd just gotten back from riding a bull at the NFR, during the crowning of Miss Rodeo America in Las Vegas. It was a very special honor for me to have had the opportunity to be a part of that.

I showed up at this event to find that, instead of bulls, they had roping steers for us to ride. Great. Not only would my rope not fit, but they were too small and skinny to ever buck under our weight. But I kept my mouth shut, kept to myself, and went about my business.

When it came time for me to ride, the announcer began this long, overblown introduction about me riding a bull at the National Finals Rodeo in Las Vegas. I don't even know how he knew; I didn't tell him. Well, I'm hearing all this while I'm getting down on my three-hundred-pound, slab-sided, razor-backed steer. I have to admit, I thought I was way too good to waste my time at this backyard punkin'-jumpin'. I didn't even recognize that I was getting too big for my britches. Oh, how God has a way of setting us up!

I nodded for the gate—the steer WALKED out—and I rolled off like a watermelon on a rail fence! The crowd went hilariously wild with laughter!

People were beating themselves laughing at the whole ordeal. I don't ever remember being more humiliated in my entire life! But you know what I am MOST embarrassed over? Instead of just taking that "bitter pill" and learning from it, I was more intent on salvaging my reputation (as if I had one to salvage). I ran to the stock contractor and asked him to run another one in the chute for me. I would show them! Problem was, I already had. I just wasn't smart enough to recognize it.

I didn't get on anything else that night, and I don't ever remember feeling so utterly clumsy, stupid, and mistreated as I felt then. Months went by, and I could think about that incident and still feel a twinge of pain. But it did me good. It made me look at a part of myself that I wouldn't have been willing to look at otherwise. Pride is a terrible thing, and it can slip into our attitude unnoticed.

I have also come to realize that how I perform in any area of my life bears no reflection on my worth as an individual. If I place my value in accordance to my performance and I do bad, I'm depressed. If I do good, I begin to think I'm "all that and a bag of chips!" That makes me like a thermometer, where I am up or down depending on my circumstances. God wants us to be more like a thermostat, where we set the temperature instead of being moved by it! We can remain steadfast in Him, whether our performance is hot or cold.

And those people in the stands poking fun and criticizing? They will always be there. Don't worry about them. Armchair quarterbacks have never won a game.

Winning a round at Fort Smith, AR 1986

SUPERMAN RETURNS

While visiting with some friends the other day, they related a story about a time when they were babysitting our sons. We were at a conference, and this couple had taken our boys to a nice restaurant to eat with them. During the evening, Colt and Tyger had to go to the bathroom, and our friends sat at the table waiting for them. Out came the boys, running through the restaurant with the paper toilet seat covers around their necks, and the middle flap part waving in the back as their cape. They were Superman! My friends laugh whenever this memory is brought up—how Tyger and Colt drew the attention of the entire restaurant as a wave of smiles and chuckles followed them all the way back to their table. It's funny how little boys' imaginations could turn paper seat covers into Superman capes! Why? Because little boys dream of being superheroes.

By the time Tyger graduated high school, he had turned in applications to several military academies, but West Pont was the one he had his heart set on. The day came when Tyger's dream came true; he received West Point's letter of acceptance. He's since gone on to serve our country for several years in the army.

I am <u>proud</u> of our military! Our soldiers deserve our utmost respect and support for the great sacrifices they have made for our country and our freedom. Thank God for our young men and women. And thank God for all you mothers and fathers who read this article and shed a tear as you remember when <u>your</u> little one was running through the house with a towel for a Superman cape. Now your "baby" might be somewhere overseas…hot, tired, lonely, and <u>determined</u> to make a difference in this world because that's who he or she IS—a defender of freedom! Know this, Mom and Dad, many of us are praying for the safety of your child. You may waltz back into your memories and see an image of a dirty faced, toothless smile…but we look at your sons and daughters serving in the military and we really do see Superman.

Tyger Tuff still can't seem to let go of his super hero identity. Here he is as Captain America. What can I say? Boys!

Skiing on West Point's slopes. Tyger liked the way the scarf tied around his head would blow as he sailed down the mountain. Whatever floats your boat! (Still a remnant of the toilet seat cape if you ask me.)

CHILI ROLLED BY A CHICKEN

Watching animals is one of my favorite calming pastimes.

We had four kittens at the barn who were just getting brave enough to venture out of the feed room and into the vast expanse of universe called the alley way. One of the kittens made the delighted discovery that an older chick (which to the kitten must have looked like a giant bird) would run from him. It's gotta be a great boost to one's confidence when something twice your size fears you!

The kitten was having a blast maneuvering the chicken around a bale of hay. While this was going on, another kitten—much smaller in size—was bravely making its debut venturing outside the feed room, just in time to get chili rolled by a crazed chicken squawking in terror as it fled the barn. The poor little kitten left scratch marks in the concrete as it fled back to the safety of the furthest, darkest corner of the feed room! What a rude response at its first attempt to venture out into life.

While I felt for the kitten, I couldn't help but chuckle all morning over its humor. We know what the kitten doesn't; it will grow larger, overcome the emotional set back, and, in time, not even notice the things that before sent it reeling in fear back to its dark corner. The truth is, venturing out into life is NOT safe! But THE most dangerous thing any of us could do after life chili rolls us is to retreat to our dark corners and wave the white flag! Life is to be LIVED…and we can't live it if we're waiting for the insurance policy that guarantees we won't lose, get hurt, be freight-trained, etc. If that little kitten was to never venture out again and it remained in that dark corner, it would never grow healthy, never be strong, and never experience the joys that life has to offer, all for the sake of "safety." Same with us. Life doesn't come with its insurance policy that promises we will never lose, never be hurt, and never get chili rolled by a crazed chicken. But if we don't step back out from our place of retreat, it's an automatic guarantee that we'll be crippled. Isn't it kinda amazing that sometimes what's dangerous is actually healthy and what looks safe is actually a death trap?

So maybe you can relate to that kitten right now. You had high hopes, and they were dashed. You stepped out after mustering up the best of your courage, and you got freight-trained. You gave something your very best shot, and you were sideswiped by something that equates to that of a crazed chicken mucking out the kitten. Okay, so you're in your dark corner right now: clear away the feathers…tell God how you feel… ask Jesus to give you renewed hope and courage…then step back out. What matters is not how *great* you become, but that you simply become! Before you know it, you're going to be so strong, and the giants that used to send you running in fear, you'll instead be eating for breakfast! Giants are to be overcome! Giants are the food of champions! What was sent to defeat you can become the stepping-stone to your next promotion.

Step out, face your fear, overcome adversity, and feast on giants!

**Cowboy Church in the Budweiser Events Center
at Larimer County, CO PRCA Rodeo**

Dumb Thoughts That Lead to Dumber Actions

It was years ago at a PRCA rodeo in East Texas. I was part of the team that put on this particular stock contractor's events. I had a good little stock dog, and we used him quite regularly during the bull riding. It worked out well…I would simply be mounted and stationed near the pickup men with my dog sitting by my horse. Once the cowboy was off the bull and all was clear, I would simply sic my dog and he'd get after the bull until the bull went through the let-out gate; then he'd come trotting back to where I was and wait for the next round. I had gotten real proud of how he worked and loved being a part of the action.

I don't remember just why I wasn't mounted at this particular rodeo, but one bull was holding up the whole show. He was big and mad and not budging. I ran to get my dog and "save the day." As I was heading down to where the action was, a man yelled at me that the arena was a "no-climb fence." I heard what the man said, but never **"*heard*"** him, if you know what I mean. In other words, I had an agenda and wasn't listening. I was the cool cowgirl with the even cooler dog, and I was on a mission to show this rodeo crowd just how cool I really was! Two stupid decisions were about to collide. One of which was, how dumb is it to build a rodeo arena with no climb fencing?! AND what's even DUMBER is to ignore that fact and walk into it while an exceedingly ticked-off bull is looking for something to drill a hole in! In my self-exalted exuberance, I headed for the bull…on foot…with my dog.

A friend of mine just recently described me as going through life with my hair on fire…always thinking about what's next and never fully living in the moment I'm in. Well, that describes this idiotic moment… hair on fire. The dog went bouncing out to the bull, got his attention, and (for whatever reason) came bouncing back to me…bringing the bull with him. I did what any "smart" blonde would do…I ran for the fence! Problem was, I couldn't get the toe of my boot into the fence to boost myself over. I remember thinking, *Ohhh!! NO-CLIMB fence! THAT'S what he meant!*

I'm scrambling and going nowhere…the crowd is literally screaming…the bull is charging and I'm about to be a human waffle. Several men had jumped down to the fence and were reaching over to get me. The pickup men had just enough time to throw one loop…it worked…and they stopped the bull just feet from me. Arms were reaching over the fence and in a collective effort they literally pulled me up and over. I was so humiliated. I didn't show off any more at that rodeo…my chili was thoroughly cooled! I took a razzing for weeks after that and deserved every bit of grief I got.

God is so good at saving the ignorant. How many times have I headed into something, totally ignoring the warnings, stampeding toward trouble with both guns blazing! We hear, but we don't HEAR. That's what Jesus meant when He said, "He who has ears to hear…let him hear." Sometimes we make decisions that place us behind a "no-climb fence," and no matter how hard we try, we can't get ourselves out. That's when we need to cry out to Jesus. He still reaches down…He still pulls people out and over. It's embarrassing sometimes to see where we are, but not admitting our stupidity in the matter simply keeps us trapped. Once we've put ourselves there, the only way out is from above.

Singing at AJRA Finals, Sweetwater, TX
Photo by David Jennings Photography

Church Service at Miles City, MT
Bucking Horse Sale Weekend 2015

MAN WHOOPINGS

Because there weren't many entries in Sr. bulls and saddle broncs, another guy along with my son were able to supply the bucking stock for our local AJRA rodeo. Colt Wrangler had a really nice little bull that came with the name "Mighty Mo." Mo was the perfect practice bull. He always turned back…hard…and might reverse it. He didn't have a set pattern that was predictable so it made a fellow have to ride correctly. If you thought he would go one way and threw yourself over there, he'd simply go the opposite direction and leave you with nothing but air between you and the ground. Mo was also EASY to handle. His great love in life was FOOD, and he'd eat out of your hand. All the guys who got on practice bulls around here loved him.

Well, the weekend was going good. The saddle bronc mare we brought bucked off a young college student, Mo bucked off one boy and was the winning ride for another one. The last day, a young man drew a bull that hipped himself on the chute, and he bailed out and called for a re-ride. Even after he got awarded a re-ride, he was still acting mad and bad-mouthing the rodeo, the stock…everything. Frankly, I don't even know why he got a re-ride. He had a fair shot at covering that bull; he just didn't and used the bull hitting his hip on the chute as an excuse. He was the typical, "I think I'm bad and it's cool looking to act mad about everything." The "I'm too good for this place" kind of person. You know the type. They're around everywhere. Well, Mo was his re-ride bull. Even after getting his way, this kid was still acting as if the world owed him something. Wonder where he learned that behavior? Wouldn't be his parents, would it?

Well, all the local bull riders were secretly rooting for Mo, as this kid was still running his mouth and acting like a peacock on steroids. He nodded, and Mo came around. About the time this kid thought he had Mo conquered, Mo reversed it and drilled him like a yard dart. It's amazing how a simple butt drilling can put things back into perspective. That kid needed a whooping but was too old for such…so he had to take a "man whooping." Mo spanked him, and all the local boys were grinning like peach-eating boars. It was a beautiful day in the neighborhood. Trying to be nice to this kid didn't do it…giving him what he wanted didn't do it…it took a butt kicking from a little sawed-off bovine to get it done. The boy picked up his rope, shut his mouth, and went home. Man whoopings… sometimes they're just what the doctor ordered.

Mo got some extra grain that night.

Colt Wrangler on his practice bull Mighty Mo

Transitions Are Tough

I always hated the area between having my feet firmly planted on the ground and my butt firmly planted in the saddle when mounting an unbroke colt. It was that place of vulnerability, where if something was thrown at me, I was in no position to handle it with grace. I've seen men who could do it with ease, but that was never the case for me. I always held one by the cheek of his bridle just in case he blew; I could at least have his head pulled around where I had some semblance of control. Of course, a horse's neck being much stronger than my arm…could actually have me slung out of there like flicking a booger off your finger… but I felt better with his head pulled around just the same. There's a point in there where you gotta go one way or the other. One leg is in midair… the horse is making his move…are you going to commit yourself to handling this next level, or are you going to step back down where it's safer…more controllable…predictable…and no ground gained.

Transitions in life can be just as unsettling as mounting an unbroke colt.

The next stage is unpredictable and you can't possibly know for sure if you got what it takes to handle the ride. You have no way of knowing if the ride is going to be smooth, or if some treacherous maneuver lays ahead of you. That's where I've kinda figured out that our attitude decides our direction…if we're self-preserving…too fearful of loss or pain…we back down to the previous level and until we change that inner attitude, that's where we'll remain. No one wants to have "self" hung out to dry, so to speak; but if preserving self—that is "what's in it for me" prevails, it will always have the strength to choke down any ability to face the unknown, unless there's a guarantee of personal success stapled to it. Don't know about you, but I've found that that guarantee doesn't exist. If you think you have one…it's a forgery.

Transitions are kinda like stepping into a dark hallway…if you don't go there, you're stuck in this one room on this one level…but if you DO go…where might it lead you? Someone rightly described transitions as "hell in the hallway." Some transitions are a result of our choosing and some are decided for us…we were comfortably seated with our cup of coffee and something threw us out into the dark hallway and locked the door behind us! The choice then has been removed…like it or not, your butt is IN the saddle and the quicker you and I decide to handle this ride… the better it goes for us. I don't like transitions…I DEFINITELY don't like them when they have been decided for me! BUT…this I truly KNOW… the Lord is not only waiting for me on that next level…He's WITH ME while I'm trying to maneuver my way through that dark, scary hallway.

John Wayne said it well, "Courage is being scared to death, but saddling up anyway." So…grab the cheek of that bridle and make the commitment to go forward. Yep…you <u>might</u> get bucked off…but you'll survive, learn from it, and hopefully get back on. Anyone can live on the ground…but those who do miss out on the joy of the ride!

**Turning a barrel on Strider at
Barrels For Angels, Marshall, TX 2016**

A Bucking Horse + Drunk People = A Miracle

I was asked to come sing horseback on the street during the Miles City, Montana, Bucking Horse Sale Weekend, a yearly event that brings thousands of people into this out of the way Montana town. Friday and Saturday nights, the Main Street is blocked off as multiple bands are crisscrossed from one another for about a half-mile stretch. The street is filled with a sea of people drinking and dancing for as far as you can see. We were on the very end of that long row of bars and bands, and I was to do an hour-long concert under the flashing lights of the intersection, followed by a live band doing an hour, and then me doing a final hour.

My horse got sick, and I was forced to borrow one. Friends searched and searched and finally found one that a bar owner had. It was a little gray gelding he roped on from time to time, but he hadn't been ridden in months and had NEVER been to town…much less seen anything like what he was going to have to endure. I spent a few minutes several blocks away on a grassy spot loping some circles, feeling him out, and praying over him. He just had a little bit of pitch in him but settled down pretty easily.

The little guy did great the first set. Not many horses like to be in front of a literal wall of speakers approximately seven feet high, that were pounding out sound so hard you feel it hitting you in the chest. By the time I was ending up the second set, this little guy had had it with me and the entire situation! You certainly couldn't blame him! He began to rear in the front end and buck up in the rear. Kinda like a mini replica of the Lipizzaner leap they do so beautifully, but this was just sheer frustration in manifestation. Poor guy! I couldn't blame him. He had put up with so much and had taken it all in stride, but he was FINISHED!

I was singing the last song of the night. Several of us had prayed that God would do something supernatural and bring about a manifestation of His presence over the crowd, but nothing, absolutely nothing, had happened. I was so disappointed. Thousands of people there, and we were being ignored successfully by the masses, with only a few stopping to listen throughout the night. About halfway through that last song as the little horse was doing his Lipizzaner imitation, and I'm working at finding ANYTHING that will cause him to settle for just two more minutes so I can finish this song as smoothly as possible, I have this thought run through my brain, "Lay the reins on his neck and stand up in the saddle."

Well...my momma didn't raise a TOTAL FOOL! That was THE STUPIDEST thought EVER!! I dismissed it as a blonde moment and kept singing. But the thought came again. This time I noticed a sort of..."authority" about it, so I started talking to God in my head while singing the song.

By the end of this inner discussion I was having, while my heart was pounding in fear, adrenaline, craziness...all the above...I had felt it just MIGHT BE GOD saying, "DO this!"

I thought, "Oh, God, if it's NOT You, this is really gonna HURT!!"

Being face planted on pavement is NOT my idea of a good ending to a concert!! But it FELT like it was God, so I breathed a last prayer, laid the reins over his neck (while he's still kicking up), took my foot out of the stirrup, and suddenly...I felt the little horse breathe a deep, easy breath. Omgosh!! It WAS God!! I stood up on the saddle and sang the last few lines of "I Pledge Allegiance to the Lamb," while that little horse stood stone still!!

But beyond the miracle of this little horse standing like a statue, another miracle was about to take place. Suddenly the sea of people started pointing and shouting, "Look, look!" And the crowd quickly shifted to where we were. Then with NO ONE saying anything at all, I was just singing the last few lines of the song, and men started saying, "I need to be saved!" People started coming under conviction and crying all over the place, and intercessors moved in to lead them to the Lord in prayer. It was nothing short of supernatural!! I was told while I was standing up on the horse, a well-meaning drunk came up behind and slapped that little horse hard on the butt...TWICE...and he never flinched!! God was holding all things together!! He truly does all things well!!

It's crazy how God may ask you to do the most outlandish things! But if it truly IS God and not our own craziness, He releases a manifestation of His presence when we obey! I'm still amazed, many years later, about that night. Why ask me to do such a risky (crazy) act that has nothing to do with drawing people to Him? I honestly don't know why. But I have learned that sometimes we must risk in order to obey. God is a God Who truly honors courage and obedience! And oh my gosh, what a display of God's hand upon it all!! I could've "safetied up" that night and went to bed disappointed, wondering why God hadn't done anything that we'd prayed for. That night would've become a distant, foggy memory to me. But one simple (scary) act of hearing and TRUSTING God made all the difference!

Miles City, MT Bucking Horse Sale Weekend concert

Working Out the Knots

I hadn't started a colt in a loooong time, and I was actually kind of excited about getting to start Strider's first colt, "Seven." Within five rides, we were venturing outside the arena where a whole new world of "boogers" exist. Seven was doing great, and I had a couple of events in Alabama and Mississippi, so it was a great opportunity to haul him along with Strider and get him acclimated to all kinds of new sights, sounds, and experiences. I had opportunities to ride him in a few state parks that had horse trails, so he could experience more than the inside of an arena. By the time we got back from that trip, it was time to up the game.

Horses are pretty much like us in some ways. When they're young and untested, they will have their imaginary boundaries; if you never push them past those, you will have a horse that will be willing to do so much…but no more. He will be a perfect angel as long as you don't mess with his Kool-Aid. But if you start expecting more from him than he thinks he should give, oh brother, the fangs come out! I sometimes call it a "knot." You know, like when a massage therapist finds that tight spot in your neck or shoulders and that's where they immediately camp. Everything feels GOOD until they start attacking those knots!

Well, that's kinda what we have to do when riding those young horses. You find the knot…that spot where they say, "Uh-uh! I'm DONE here!" One of the best ways I know to bring those knots to the surface is by loping circles. You can walk and trot nice big circles, and all will be fine. But up the speed one notch and start loping, and whatever knots are in there will surely work their way to the surface! Course, in all honesty, I can't blame them. I HATE going in circles—in the arena AND in life. The colt has to think, "This makes NO SENSE! We're going NOWHERE! My rider must be an idiot! I'm DONE with this!" And they grab the bit, or simply just stiffen their neck and blow off down the pen, hoping to escape the tyranny of it all.

I don't know about you, but I've done the same thing. I have found myself in situations that made NO SENSE to me at all!! I would be going nowhere…just flying a sort of holding pattern, not going ANYWHERE but seemingly never landing anyplace in particular either. I've grabbed the bit and tried to make things happen in the hope of it getting me out from where I was. Every time I did this, I (just like that colt) had to circle LONGER—until I would surrender, quit, grabbing the bit and instead, YIELD to the pressure that I was under! Once that colt quits fighting and yields to what we're asking, we release the pressure and reward him with REST. That's exactly how God handles us. Once we quit fighting Him and YIELD, He rewards us with rest. God is gonna put pressure on our knots, I can guarantee it! Might as well yield to Him, because it's always about making us a better person and bringing us to a place where He can reward us with greater blessings! When you can't make any sense out of where you are, that's when you need to trust Him most! Let Him work that knot out…REST will immediately follow.

SMOKING HOT JEEPS AND FRESH STARTS

I had an '83 Jeep for twelve years after buying it when it was already ten years old. Nothing…not a dent, scratch…NOTHING ever happened to that Jeep. That Jeep finally spit the bit, and I decided to buy a brand-new Jeep, already lifted four inches and set up for "pretend" rock crawling. It was black…SHINY BLACK. My first brand-new Jeep EVER!! Not long after getting it, a horse decided to run his upper teeth over the hood, just to see how black tasted, I guess. Then Tyger, while "fixing fence," flipped it in a pasture after an airborne jump that landed horribly wrong. Funny how fixing fence called for off-road, dirt-racing maneuvers.

If that wasn't enough, Colt Wrangler, in his senior year, asked to just drive to the Llano River to watch it on the rise. With me knowing better, I strongly advised him to be sure and NOT drive out on the gravel bar, but simply watch it from the ridge…and be back in an hour. Parents…we should know better than to turn a teenage boy loose, with a cool Jeep, among other teenage boys with four-wheel-drive rigs, down on a river that's rising from all the flood rains.

One hour passed…no son…two hours…nothing. Finally at 1:00 a.m., a truck pulls up and deposits Colt Wrangler at the front door and leaves (I would've left fast too). Sure enough, Colt had done exactly what I said NOT to do and drove the Jeep out onto the gravel bar and sunk it! If there's ever any retribution for his disobedience, it's the fact that he had worked for HOURS trying to get it unstuck. Not to mention the gnawing fear of death over what was facing him by placing my precious Jeep in harm's way! After expressing myself CLEARLY the importance of him praying to God that the river not rise up into my Jeep (as that it might drastically affect the length of his young life), I sent him to bed. Long before daylight, we got up, got shovels, tow rope, and were down on the Llano to see if my Jeep was still above water. I felt like the king coming to see Daniel in the lion's den and hoping against hope that he was still alive. Was my Jeep safe? It was!! We got busy digging, filling ruts, and with a borrowed tractor, got it pulled out as water was filling up the holes behind us…literally! By the time we got fully out, we were in waist-deep water! Nothing like this EVER happened to my old Jeep! Why was all this happening to the only Jeep I ever bought new?? It's a mystery… But I think the same thing goes for making a new start in life. As long as we're going the "old way," we may not like the results but at least they're usually predictable. But let us make a bold new start, a change for the positive, and WHAM, we can be hit with some unexpected stuff! Make the shift toward a new start and living right, and suddenly you've become a target. But just like my Jeep, you can dig out of any rut and move on. So don't be afraid of a new move, a new job, a new relationship, a new you!! Will you face new problems? Most definitely…but let me tell ya, it's WORTH it!! And by the way, Colt Wrangler Rhino-Lined my Jeep inside and out! She may not be new anymore, but she is still SMOKING HOT!!

**Colt Wrangler surprised me by having
Rhino-Lined my Jeep inside and out!**

Focus

Where we focus our attention is what multiplies in our lives. Think about it. Where our thoughts go, we go. What dictates our attention directs our path. Even in the simplest of situations. For instance, a barrel racer must focus on the pocket, NOT the barrel. Why? Because where their eyes go, their hands direct. A rough stock rider MUST keep his eyes focused at the correct place on the animal he's riding to be able to keep his body in the right position to stay aboard. You'll sometimes see a bull rider looking out just before he bucks off. What happened? Inwardly he wanted out…his look betrayed his inner desire and his body followed suit.

Focus is a powerful thing!! Focus in the positive develops passion… and passion is POWER. Focus in the negative builds thought processes of defeat that set a person up for perpetual failure. We literally can sabotage our own future by allowing negative thought processes to take over our thinking. To keep our focus positive takes EFFORT because everything about this world, left to itself, tends toward chaos and decay. As I often say, "ANY dead fish can float downstream; it takes a LIVE one to go against the current!" To keep your focus "clean" takes consistent effort and discipline in our thought life.

Ted Nuce once told me how when he was believing to win the world title in bull riding, he would consistently "see" himself as such; and immediately after a buck off, he'd tell himself, "This is not who I am, I'm a world champion!" He won that title in 1985.

Many have heard Lynn McKenzie's testimony when she won the world title in barrels on Magnolia Missile. She didn't even get to make that many rodeos because of teaching school, and she found herself at the NFR. Feeling overwhelmed by all this, she leaned on her friendship with Jesus and focused on Him. Before running down the alleyway, she'd ask Jesus to put His hands in hers, put His feet in her feet, and ride Missile through her. She placed or won every round! Well…every round except one. About the fourth round, she thought, "I've got this" and didn't focus on Jesus riding through her. She didn't place in that round. After that, she repented, placed her focus back on the One Who had gotten her there (you know…"dance with the one who brought you"), made money every round after that, and also won the world title that year. Focus… where our thoughts go, we go!

This truth reigns in all aspects of life. Where our focus goes, we go. Concerning end times, Luke 21 records Jesus telling some of the signs of this age. Signs that are prevalent in our generation, but verse 26 says something powerful about our focus: "Men's hearts failing them for fear and for looking after those things which are coming on the earth." When our focus is earthbound, the result will be FEAR.

During 2016, I began to be fearful over what I saw in the coming elections. With my thoughts earthbound, I saw no good options. When I realized where my focus was, I turned my focus heavenward to hear God's perspective. I was not disappointed. Surprised…but not disappointed. God spoke to me more than once about HIS pick for our nation, and hearing from Him personally, I had great confidence and hope was renewed instead of being fearful. I refused to get my information from news media after that and kept my focus heavenward. I had PEACE while many were (and still are) fearful and even angry. Focus is a POWERFUL thing…for good or evil. Pay attention to what and where your focus is. For what directs our focus, directs us!

PRCA Rodeo, Huron, SD 1986

DOUGHNUT HOLES?

Have you ever noticed how horse manure that's been covered in red dirt can look an awful lot like doughnut holes rolled in cinnamon? One guy from Colorado said, "No," when I asked this once. He must've never cleaned up horse manure in Oklahoma! Horse manure rolled in red dirt has an amazing resemblance to cinnamon-coated doughnut holes. Well…hello…you could easily judge this scenario by the surroundings! Horse manure isn't offered in doughnut shops, and doughnuts aren't manufactured in barnyards. It's smart to take into consideration the surroundings, but I've seen some terrific individuals who were found in a bar, and some pretty sorry counterfeit individuals who were discovered in church! Fact is, some things are not always what they seem…so it's smart to sometimes step back and ask for the wisdom of God in a matter before "taking a bite."

How many times have we heard horror stories of people who dated a Cinderella or Prince Charming, only to discover too late that they married something more attune to a horror movie than a fairy tale? Horse manure rolled in red dirt.

God knows what's in the heart, what's under the hood, what's hidden in the fine print, what's REALLY inside that beautifully wrapped opportunity. I had an experience once where I "heard" on the inside of me these words, "It's a one-way street."

That was an expression I had never used nor even thought of before, but I immediately knew what it meant—someone who only takes but never gives back. With that phrase, I also had a face flash in my mind. I thought, "What a cool line for a song!" So I wrote the song that morning, and time eventually revealed it was also exactly right concerning the person whose face I saw.

God is just so cool!! He LOVES to give us insight that we have no way of knowing without His help. He WANTS us to ask. Matter of fact, His Word says, "We have not because WE ask not." God DESIRES to partner with us and give us insight that we can't have without Him. Truth is, we weren't meant to go through life independent of God. Scripture says that all things were created BY Him, FOR Him, and IN Him all things consist. Sounds a lot like He's the CENTER, doesn't it? How well can anyone expect to go through life void of the CENTER of their being?

I've made enough mistakes in my life that ended up costing dollars—and years! I REALLY don't want to continue making similar mistakes. But I know that I can easily be duped if I'm standing on my own intelligence alone. No, thank you. If I order a meal and it isn't what I'd hoped it'd be, once I take a bite, I'll be a little disappointed, but no big deal. But investing thousands of dollars in something that flops…or giving your heart away to someone behind a pretty mask that's covering up the monster within…that's something NONE OF US have the time or the heart or money for!!

So why not start building a relationship with Jesus NOW? What a waste to live a life without tapping into the genius that's being offered to us!! Mistakes will always be made, but none so drastic as a life lived void of its CENTER. Open up just a little and offer Jesus the honest vulnerability of your heart and He'll reveal Himself to you. I promise He will. It sure beats a life of constant trial and error, and worse, an eternity where no recourse is offered!

Bottom line, I LOVE the fact that NOTHING is hid from the eyes and knowledge of my Father! I can't see beneath the surface, but HE sees all, and He is MORE than willing to share any insight I may need in a particular situation. Why go through life only seeing what's on the surface and, therefore, being vulnerable to all that's devious? Don't just bite into anything that looks pretty; make it a practice to ask for God's take on it before making your move. Anybody up for some cinnamon-coated doughnut holes???

SLOTTED

I have this mental system. Whether it's a right thing to do or not, I'm not entirely sure, but it seems to work for me. I have "slots" for people. Say for instance, I come across someone who promises to be able to do something, but in actuality, they never back up what they say. After that happens a few times, you realize that they have a great talk, but you simply cannot put your trust in them to actually DO what they say. So in my mind, into a particular slot they go. Their slot may be titled something like this: "Enjoy their company but put NO WEIGHT in what they say." Or if I'm looking for a one-word title, it might be "Undependable." The reason I do this is to keep my emotions from being disturbed and being angry with them. That way, once I have established in my mind the fact that they will never come through with the goods, I stop being disappointed with them as a person. I've slotted them in that pigeonhole that keeps them further from my heart. I can, therefore, enjoy that person's personality but keep myself free from the wrecks they invariably will cause.

It's like some horses we've had. Some we could count on through thick and thin and some…well, you know. I figure it this way: every person has their place. Very possibly, NOT the place God intends for them to be, but a place created by their own choices; it's where they seem to reside. I am NOT their integrity police; therefore, if I have no authority to demand change in those areas…I "slot them" and move on. That way, I am not having to deal with inner anger every time they are around, and I SURE DON'T put myself in a position where I'm hung out to dry if they don't come through.

Like that horse you may have owned at one time, you know the one! I owned one of those. I had him from a baby, and at eight years old, he still could swallow his head for no apparent reason and drill you like a yard dart. He was a cool horse, but you just could NOT put your trust in him enough to ever relax! You have to "slot" the horses you can and cannot do certain things on if you want to continue riding without getting into a wreck! Finally at fifty years old (me, not the horse), I was riding him one day and kept feeling that knot in his back. Reality FINALLY broke through the fog in my brain, and I said, "WHY am I still riding this horse??!!" I got off him that moment before he acted on what was obviously running through his mind. I called a PRCA stock contractor who tried him and bought him; he earned a place bucking in the contractor's "A" string for a few years.

I placed the horse in his correct slot, and I was no longer agitated by his behavior! It's amazing how that works. I have a friend who has a saying about ordeals that are outside her circle of influence: "This isn't my circus, and those aren't my monkeys." It pays to know a horse before you put your foot in the stirrup…and it pays to know a person's character before you hitch your wagon to them. Not everyone deserves your trust! We can save ourselves from a few wrecks in life if we pay attention and take note of people's patterns because in reality, you didn't "slot" them… they did that themselves. You simply recognized it.

Are You Collected?

I once owned a REALLY BIG three-year-old quarter horse stallion. When I first started riding him, he was SO ROUGH it was MISERABLE! It felt like riding a log truck with a flat tire. He was all strung out. He started getting broke at the poll, and the ride became amazingly smoother! Why? Because he got collected.

We're like that. We get sprawled out, scattered—and the ride gets really rough. Why? We're not collected. We're involved in too many things, going in too many directions. Matter of fact, many people lack an overruling "anchor" of sorts that holds them steady and is a "compass" for the direction of their life. They're like a flock of birds that move erratically in different directions, without purpose—or purpose lost. Either way, the result is we're not together, we're not "collected," and so the "ride" we're on gets rough!

How do we fix it? Same way we do a horse. The way we get a horse collected and broke at the poll is by getting him "soft," "yielded," responding to the pressure of the rein instead of resisting it. How yielded are you to the hand of God? Do you quickly yield to the touch of the Master, or do you resist it? Many people want a smooth ride in life while they are too scattered, too involved in things that are not conducive to a walk with God and resisting His leadership. It's not going to happen. The only way for our life to have purpose and meaning, not to mention direction, is to quit moving according to our own desire. God has a plan for your life! He wants to take you somewhere. He has a goal, a destination in mind, but He can't take us there unless we yield. Let go of some things that you shouldn't be a part of. Let go of some things in your heart—i.e., past mistakes, hurts, injustices, failures, and disappointments. You can't hold on to these things and still have purpose. It'll suck all the life out of you. It's past. Let it go! Take your focus off what's behind you, collect yourself, and move forward! Allow God to pull you together. You'll not just come under yourself, <u>He'll</u> come under you! You'll be amazed at how much smoother the ride will become!

Singing at the Loveland, CO Pro Rodeo Cowboy Church. Not every horse is smooth enough to sing on while loping. Strider is a smooth operator!

INNER OR OUTER BEAUTY?

From time to time, we'll buy a horse that's been kept in a lot or a stall. They always look great! They're so clean and well groomed. It's wonderful to just look at 'em. Well, we bring the horse home and turn him out in the coastal field with the other horses. It's great to watch. They run and buck, get their pecking order worked out, and find their best buddy. In the process, they get introduced to chickens, ducks, wild animals, and cattle. Some of these horses have never seen any of these things! It's a whole new world for them, a world outside the tiny confines of their former existence. There is SO MUCH to learn. They don't know any better than to booger at some of the safest things and walk right up to some of the most dangerous things! They've got to learn how to maneuver their feet in rough terrain (something they've never had to do). They have to learn everything from handling themselves in a herd, to avoiding the prickly pear, and lots more—not to mention long days of working cattle, hours of being tied, and oh yes, lots of wet saddle pads. It's wonderful for them. They get to be a horse, and they learn tons.

Problem is, they don't <u>look</u> like they used to look! What used to be a flawless coat now has some bite marks. Their coat is layered with dirt from those good ole times of playing in the pond, followed by a wonderful roll in the dirt. It's much harder to keep that nice overall "plushy fat" appearance. Their mane isn't as beautifully thick and well-groomed as before. But boy, are they ever happy! And you can take them out and count on them to hold together on you when the pucker factor gets intense! You aren't having to ride them with the mind-set of keeping them out of a possible wreck—you can ride them with the mind-set of being able to count on <u>them</u> to keep <u>you</u> out of a wreck!! You see, inner strength and good character cannot be instilled without messing up outer appearances. Oh, that outward beauty can easily be gotten back—but what they've gained in knowledge will never be taken from them and is priceless. An inner beauty has been instilled—but for a time, it cost some in the outer appearance department. I've seen people who have been in trying situations, and instead of seeking to do the <u>right thing</u>, they're only interested in saving face. They're more concerned with how they look than building character. It's like parents who will do whatever it takes to buy their kids out of trouble instead of allowing them to pay the price for their actions. Good character doesn't come without a price. For example, many marriages <u>could</u> be saved if both would be willing to drop the facade, open up to those who could help, and go to the <u>root</u> of the problem. The list is endless. Sometimes it can get a little messy and uncomfortable and ugly, but by doing the right thing, we build integrity and strength of character, and the inner beauty gained is <u>priceless</u>!

Performing on Strider is always FUN!!
Photo by David Jennings Photography

JOE COOL

Back when we were on the road full time, going from rodeo to rodeo, we'd often stop at friends' houses between events.

One such time we were at a good friend's house for a couple of days. Our friend had several fighting cocks running wild around the place. As a joke, he caught one, tied a string to its leg, and tied it inside the trailer with the horse. Joe was beating himself, laughing as we pulled out of their drive. The rooster was bouncing off the roof of the trailer, and the horse trailer was rocking, with the horse jerking his head around to dodge the rooster. A few days and several hundred miles later, we found the horse and rooster getting along quite well. We named him "Joe Cool" in honor of his "donor," and Tyger, who was only four at the time, took to making him his personal pet. I really didn't think he'd get it done, but by golly, in a few weeks, Tyger was pulling around his little red wagon with Joe Cool (untied and free) contented to ride in it!

We had more fun with that rooster. We'd pull up on the rodeo grounds, unload the horse, and out would strut Joe Cool, ready to check out his new surroundings. He'd mill around the grounds, scratching in the horse and cow manure, and at dusk he'd find his way back through the maze of trailers to "his" trailer and roost for the night. During the wee hours of the morning, anyone camping on the grounds could hear Joe Cool crowing (rooster crows are greatly magnified when coming from the inside of a metal trailer). He was quite the conversation piece, to say the least. People wanted to know WHY we were hauling a rooster!

Isn't it crazy, the things that leave their imprint on us? We go through life and leave our fingerprints everywhere along the way and never know the effect that our touch has on other people. But they remember. Those years were good, but a very trying season in our lives. Colt was newborn, money was scarce, and the pressures were intense. One crazy joke ended up being such a "comic relief" in our life at a time it was greatly needed.

Make a difference in someone's day…today. Sow seeds of kindness. They cost so little to sow, and they bring forth such a rich and enduring harvest! Now, years later, when I think back on those times, I can't even recall the incidents that, at the time, seemed to be so overwhelming. Yet I _do_ recall the kindness of our friends, allowing us to invade their home, cook in a _real_ kitchen, and just share our disappointments, fears, hopes, and dreams together. I remember the funny things that momentarily distracted us from the pressures…I remember Joe Cool.

**Crystal and Strider at Miles City, MT
Bucking Horse Sale Weekend 2014**

An incredible ten days exploring Italy with Tyger

The Island of Malta

I LOVED Venice!!

Venice

Exploring the southern
slopes of Italy's Alps

OVERFLOWING MOUTHS AND WATER TROUGHS

I don't know about you, but we have a problem around our house when it comes to remembering to turn off the water when filling the trough. We make promises. We tell ourselves we won't forget it THIS TIME, only to wake up to a man-made flood range, again. I always make myself feel better by saying, "Well…the ground needed watering anyway." Or this one, "The horse's feet were needing some moisture." We FINALLY admitted to ourselves we couldn't seem to handle this most basic of responsibilities and went out and bought ourselves a timer for the water hose! It's great. We set the timer and walk off in blissful peace, knowing it's dealt with. I find that running my mouth is a lot like filling the water trough. Though I start with good intentions of only saying what NEEDS to be said, I find I almost always seem to let more than enough "ooze" (more like "gush") out, and before I know it, I have just created a mud hole! I make promises. No good. I tell myself that I'm NOT going to, and that's just what I end up doing. Have you ever promised yourself that you wouldn't say a word, only to spew it all out and more within five minutes? Then I justify it by telling myself something like, "THEY probably needed to hear it, that's why it came out." Wouldn't it be so cool if someone would come up with a "timer for the mouth?" I'd pay a high price for one. (I've paid a price for the verbal overflow, as have others who were recipients of it.) The book of Proverbs says that verbal strife is like pouring water out of a jug. Once you start to pour, it's mighty hard to stop the flow.

I guess the way to handle our mouths is the same way we need to do the water trough. Just don't ever relax our watch over it! I can't afford to turn my back on my mouth for one minute! If I ever go to sleep for just a little bit, thinking I've got it "whooped," I awake to a mouth running wild and a mud hole in the making!

COWGIRL LOGIC

I have found one area to attack when seeking to keep my mouth under control, and that's my thoughts. I can't allow my thoughts to run wild and also keep a handle on my mouth. Proverbs also says that out of the abundance of the heart the mouth speaks. In other words, what I think on is what I will eventually SAY. What's in there will find expression. So it's not good enough for me to promise I'll be good, I won't. If I don't want ugly speech to come out my mouth, then I can't allow myself to dwell on ugly thoughts. If I don't want to give someone a "what for," then I can't meditate on the rotten things they've done. I've got to control it in the mental arena. Because I can promise you, if I don't, it will show up in my speech and my attitude will be one of a walking, overflowing trough that muddies up everything in its path.

PRCA Rodeo at The Nile in Billings, MT 1986

MY CLAIM TO FAME

We hadn't been doing cowboy church services at horse fairs very long at all. People were beginning to hear good things about the services, and they were growing in size, but not like such a growth that happened after this one memorable Sunday morning. I was without a horse for this service, and I had found one to borrow. He was a beautiful black quarter horse stallion. He had never been in front of speakers pounding out music before, but he was settling in nicely. I honestly don't know what came over me, but I had this sudden and incredible urge to just goof off with this one song I was singing and decided to stand up in the saddle. Ever do something WHILE you are totally aware of the fact that WHAT you are doing is "ignorance gone to seed?" This was one of those times for me. KNOWING it was stupid beyond reason, I did it anyway. I got my feet up under me in the saddle…while I'm singing…and I noticed the stud's ears "talking." My thoughts were going something like, "Better get your butt back in the saddle, girl, and quit goofing around." So…just as I was kicking MY feet out from under me, the stud did the same. My rear came down just in time to connect with the seat of the saddle as the horse's rear was coming up. It kinda catapulted me through the air. The really cool thing was, as I was sailing through the air, it just so happened that the song was at an instrumental part (I couldn't have planned that if I had tried!)

Well, I landed on my butt right when it was time to sing the last part of the song…so I did. There's no recovery at this point, so why not go on and make the best of it? The place went wild! What made it worse was to find that the three main clinicians that year were ALL at this service…Clinton Anderson, Curt Pate, and Chris Cox. OF ALL times to do something utterly stupid, why then? It's bad enough to show your ignorance publicly, but to do it in view of these guys was even more humiliating than normal. I was told…more than once…that every one of the clinicians talked about it during their presentation.

Actually, with great grace, God BLESS 'em! They could have crucified me. The next year we were there, the size of the crowd for that church service doubled! EVERYONE wanted to know if I was gonna do it again? That service still grows…though I hear mutterings from time to time about wanting to see an encore. You know, thinking back, I'm convinced God used my own ignorance for His service. Though I wouldn't want to do it again, I'm actually glad it happened. God is so awesome that He doesn't need my abilities to serve Him. He actually can use my INABILITIES just as easily. That's good to know…especially when your inabilities far outnumber your abilities! Quit fretting about what you CAN'T do and just do whatever it is you CAN do…with ALL your heart…and do it with the Lord in mind. Let HIM make of it what HE wants…and use it to whatever degree HE chooses. Some of you are known for your talents and accomplishments…use it for His glory.

Me?

Well…I can fly through the air, land on my butt, and hold a note. Cool, huh! Hey…everybody's gotta be good at SOMETHING!

**Cowboy Church at Midwest Horse Fair, Madison, WI
on a stallion called Half Pass Midnight**

THE TEST OF PRESSURE

Seems I'm always starting another colt, though I am continually saying this one's my last. When I run on to a colt that I especially like, there's one favorite trainer I send them to. I always know that the outcome will be well worth my investment.

I once took one to him, and I was pleased with what I had put on the colt already. I felt fairly confident that my trainer friend would <u>finally</u> compliment me on my work. He asked me a couple of questions:

"Do you have him thus and so?"

"Sure, sure!" I said with a confident smile.

He gets on him, moves him forward, presses a spur in him to check his softness in moving off pressure…slight delay. Did I say "slight" delay? "Sluggish resistance" is a more accurate description. He just keeps the colt moving forward while his spur remains in place. My horse starts pitching…his spur remains steady…my horse pitches harder…the spur stays. Now he's bucking. My friend is holding his foot there, WHILE he's "gouging" <u>me</u> verbally. How do they DO that? I'd be grabbing leather, my foot would long ago have left its appointed place, and I WOULDN'T be looking off at someone else and TALKING!

"YEAH, YEAH!" my friend is saying, "He's SOFT!"

"No buck!"

"Yeah, he's BROKE! Good job!"

What could I say? I just stood there with this sheepish grin…"don't have a clue"…sort of a reddish flush on my face. Thirty minutes and one wringing wet horse later, my friend has my colt moving nicer and softer than I ever did in ninety days of riding!

What I thought was a good job came apart like a two-dollar watch in thirty seconds or less! How could that be? It wasn't DEEP ENOUGH. You can always tell how deep something is by how much pressure it can withstand. Character is like that. We can ALL act good when things are going our way, but it's another thing entirely for us to hold it together when we are being pressed on all sides. That's the true test of character. Pressure tests our mettle. What we are made of—what is actually a true picture of the kind of person we are—is seen when we are "squeezed." When anything is squeezed, what it's been soaking up is what comes out.

Training horses is like training our kids as well as ourselves. If we want them to truly BE a consistent picture of good character, we can't make everything EASY! My horse knew the cues, but it hadn't gone any deeper than <u>suggestions</u>. To truly be TRAINED, it has to become second nature. My work wasn't deep enough, and it became painfully obvious under pressure.

I sometimes find myself "bucking" under the hand of God's discipline in my life. But the fact remains that if I don't allow His work within me to go <u>deeper</u>, I'll not be fit to handle the pressure that I must be able to handle in order to walk in my destiny. God is more accurate in knowing just how much pressure to apply and when to release it than the most trusted horse trainers are! If God has His spur in you right now, there's a REASON it's there! The quicker you obey, the sooner He'll release it, and you just might learn something and <u>soften</u> in the process!

T-BALL WISDOM

It was a T-ball game, a new experience for me. We were usually on the road during all the summer months, so hometown adventures as such were not our norm of experiences. Colt Wrangler was on one of the teams. While the other kids knew the ropes, Colt was placed outfield, 'cause it would take a miracle for a ball to wander out that far. Good thing…he faced backward most of the time, more interested in what might be moving in the nearby woods than what was moving on the playing field. While the other kids (and parents) were getting involved in the game, Colt was picking his nose, scratching his butt, sitting down and eating clover, etc. That's when I noticed it…that crummy feeling of embarrassment because my pride was being assaulted. I was actually becoming embarrassed because my boy wasn't one of the "good" players. (Actually, he wasn't a player at all!) What's up with that? Who made sports the defining factor of someone's worth anyway? I was ashamed of my attitude and changed it right there on the spot. I began watching other parents and was embarrassed at how they responded to their children when (horror of horrors!!) they didn't play up to their expectations! What damage we do to our children when we respond to them in anger or disappointment simply because our pride was exposed and bruised.

You know, sometimes…maybe a lot of times…we want our kids to excel for the wrong reasons. We can want our kids to be good at something in the public eye just so we don't get embarrassed. We can also want them to be good at something that we didn't get to do, trying to relive our lives through our kid's successes. Problem is, we put undue pressure on them to perform and either create a competitive monster or else totally ruin a kid's desire for something and, therefore, never see them reach their full potential…all because of our own pride and insecurity.

Every person is born with their own unique DNA. Within that DNA is a blueprint of who they are, what they like, what they were created for, etc. We've got to let our kids become who they were created to be, not try shaping them into whatever mold fits <u>our</u> personal agendas. And we've got to allow them the freedom to fail and grow and develop.

As Colt grew, he became a very gifted drummer, a pretty talented little bull rider, and a good hunter who's pretty handy with a bow and a rifle. (He'd still rather watch what's in the woods than play ball.) That's Colt...my adrenaline junkie. It's great to watch him be strong in the areas that God gifted him in. It's so much more fun to just let our kids be who they are and be their biggest supporters. You know, come to think of it...I learned a lot from watching T-ball.

Colt Wrangler's very first bike modification that got him an invitation to Austin's prestigious Hand Built Motorcycle Show.

When Colt Wrangler isn't working on motorcycles... he's usually drumming.

Colt was brought this all electric bike to see if he could make it look sleek and less blocky. This job got Colt another invite to Austin's Hand Built Show.

Awakened to Manners

Horses are great about finding their slot within the structure of the herd. Pecking order is always established, and as long as you've got a group of horses where one isn't a tyrant, everything has a smoothness to it. For whatever reason, one colt we once owned developed into a horrible tyrant. He was sweet to people, but to horses…? He was the worst I had ever seen. One time he got a mare penned up in a corner and was pounding her so hard he knocked her down and then set into kicking her while she was on the ground. I was able to get him off of her, but it was obvious we had to find some sort of solution to the problem. The solution came soon enough. We got a new gelding, and he was a huge boy. At first, he walked a wide path around "Blue," giving him top-dog status, but this didn't last long. As was always the case, Blue pushed limits, and one day he pushed too hard. That morning as all the horses came running up from the pasture to be fed, here came Blue, first as always, except for one distinct difference. He had assorted marks, plus a sort of "racing stripe" down one side of his body about two inches wide that was minus his hide and hair. Ummm, I wonder who had had enough? As the other horses filed in, there was no evidence of change until the new gelding walked in…Blue very respectfully gave way to him. The big gelding never let his authority go to his head to dog the other horses. He was an easygoing gentleman, but when he'd had enough, he'd had enough. It amazed me that Blue never hammered on the other horses after that day. I don't know how bad it had gotten, but however fierce the battle had been, it was well worth it. From that day forward, Blue had respect for others and the pasture had peace.

I love having those kind of "gentle soldiers" on our place. They are great to turn the young colts in with; they teach manners and respect. Left to themselves, young horses can become cocky and tyrannical and can develop an unteachable attitude. Turn 'em in with an old warhorse, and attitudes quickly change. When we have a young stallion, I like turning his cocky self in with an older, seasoned, bred mare. She can do WONDERS for the breeding attitude of a young stud. When breeding season comes for him, he approaches a mare asking for an invitation into her presence instead of presuming the posture of a rapist.

Yep, manners are great…in horses as well as people. No person or animal is born with manners. Manners have to be developed within by someone who demands a level of respect. Just like colts need older, stronger, and wiser horses to run with so they can learn how to live in a herd, we have a need for our sons and daughters to learn the common respect for others to live in society. Left to themselves with no one to oversee them, this never happens.

Sometimes it takes an old "war horse" to change the attitudes of a younger generation. The book of Proverbs says to discipline your son, and you'll have peace in the house. Peace within our homes and peace within our pastures…aahhh, what an amazing difference discipline makes!

Singing pre-rodeo entertainment on my sweet QH gelding Corndog, at Manawa, WI

My Favorite Christmas

Of all the umpteen Christmases I've experienced, one still stands head and shoulders above the rest. I can't even exactly express why, except to say that this one was "special"…it had the touch of God on it. Ray and I had only been married about three years; Tyger was a little more than a year old, and we were living hand to mouth…literally. For weeks, I had been setting back <u>every</u> spare penny I could get my hands on and praying that by some miracle of God, something would "happen," and we'd have the means to have a "real" Christmas. The week of Christmas came, and I had a grand total of $4 and some change to spend on our family for Christmas. The tree was easy…living at that time in the Ozarks of northern Arkansas, we had found our "perfect tree" in the woods, cut it down, and brought it home. Tyger was mesmerized by the lights and shiny ornaments. I didn't want anyone to come in and see that we had no presents, so I filled boxes with rocks and blocks of wood, wrapped them up, and placed them under the tree. Christmas Eve came, and so did a good snow the night before. The ponds were frozen thick…a beautiful snow was on the ground, and I dug out two pairs of ice skates that I had bought a couple of years before at a thrift store. I took the $4 and change to the local gas station/grocery store and bought a quart of eggnog and a half gallon of ice cream. It was a brilliant move, I thought, on how to take that small amount of money and buy a Christmas gift that the whole family could enjoy.

With Christmas taken care of and it being a gorgeous day, we donned our ice skates and spent the afternoon skating 'til we were cold and tired. We headed to the house to warm up by the wood stove and break out our Christmas ice cream and eggnog…turned on the TV and *It's a Wonderful Life* was just coming on. Ray had never seen that movie before, and it was THE PERFECT touch for such a wonderful day! (To this day, it's a family tradition to sit together and watch that movie sometime during the Christmas season…I still cry every time.) It was a WONDERFUL Christmas!! But it wasn't over yet. A neighbor came by and brought several used toys all wrapped up for Tyger. He couldn't have known those were just "dummy presents" under the tree! Then another neighbor showed up and brought us a nice big turkey to fix the next day for Christmas dinner!! By this time, we were in tears. In all our efforts, we had come up with just over $4 for Christmas, but what God did for us that day couldn't have been bought for 100 times that amount!

Isn't that what Christ-mas is all about? It's not about what we can or can't buy or do…it's what God has done for us! He not only gave His Son, Jesus, to be born in a human body so that we could experience being "born again," as Jesus Himself put it, but He's the gift that just KEEPS ON GIVING…literally. What God did for us that Christmas lingers on in my heart, because MORE than having money to buy presents, MORE than being able to do just the simplest things for ourselves, we experienced God's love for us. The atmosphere that permeated our home that year was directly from heaven itself! You can't buy that.

**Tyger
home for
Christmas!**

BE AN ORIGINAL

I find it amazing, the limits people will go to just to try and impress you that they're something they're not. What's wrong with just being who you are?! You know, YOU are the ONLY person in the entire WORLD who can be you as good as you can!! Anytime you try to be someone you're not, the very BEST you can pull off is a badly done second-place imitation. Why be an imitation when you can be an ORIGINAL? What's so wrong with you being YOU?

Back when I was riding bulls, a guy who had no idea I did such a thing was trying to impress me by saying he "used to ride bulls." (Boy, haven't we heard THAT line?) I just acknowledged him, though it was obvious by his mannerisms that he had never been a bull rider (Maybe he got on one once?), and when he opened his mouth, he removed all doubt. He told me this lengthy story of how he took this "suicide wrap" (heard that one, too), and he showed me how he did it. He wrapped the rope around his thumb. (That part was classic, though it gets even better.) Then he proceeded to tell me how the bull was so bad that the pickup men couldn't get to him to save him! (Need I say more?) It was all I could do to keep a straight face. All the while he thought he was impressing me, and he never had a clue just how ridiculous he looked. What a shame to think you have to make up a line of bull to be somebody in someone else's eyes.

I guess winning the approval of others can be so important to some that they start acting according to what they think you want them to be. It's all downhill from there. If I spend my life trying to convince people I'm something other than who I really am, then I have wasted my chance to become the person God created me to be! If I must have the approval of others, then my self-worth is wrapped up in what others think of me. That leaves my value as changeable as the stock market.

Fact is, our worth has to be established in the Lord for us to have any confidence in who we are. My value is solely God made. Therefore, though I don't enjoy rejection, it doesn't devastate me because my self-worth doesn't rest in whether or not I win your approval. I chose to go after God's approval for my actions and heart condition; therefore, I can survive if I don't win yours. What an easier path it is to travel down then trying to be all things to all people.

Be yourself, even if your talents and worldly accomplishments lined up end to end couldn't get you past your driveway! There's something about the atmosphere around a person who's completely comfortable in their own skin. They're literally a breath of fresh air in a society overwrought with an abundance of fake people.

Be who you are. Be an original. Be that "breath of fresh air" wherever you go!

WPRA Finals Lazy E Arena, Guthrie, OK 1986
Winning Rookie Of The Year in bulls and bares

POSITIONED FOR PURPOSE

We can learn so much from sports. Who hasn't experienced being inspired after watching some sports movie that brought home in graphic detail the inner courage it took to overcome? We all walk out feeling the determination to get up off the ground, dust ourselves off, and try again. Life is about trying, failing, and trying again and again. When asked how he felt about the multiple hundreds of times he had failed in his attempt to create a light bulb, Edison replied that he hadn't failed at all; he had simply discovered over a thousand ways that it couldn't be done! What an attitude!

When I first started getting on bulls and desperately wanting to learn how to ride, I borrowed some fat Hereford heifers to buck out once. We hauled them to a nearby arena, and I got on, fell off, got back on, fell off, listened to advice, got back on again, fell off again. It was TOTALLY DISCOURAGING. What made it worse was they weren't bucking hard enough to dislodge my grandmother, and I was rolling off like a watermelon on top of a rail fence! The bull rider helping me was getting frustrated at the whole situation. I remember it feeling SO HARD! It felt overwhelming at the time. The harder I tried, the worse it got. I was always playing catch up, fighting to stay afloat while behind in the game and getting beat up in the process. I don't know when it clicked, but while listening to his instructions for the umpteenth time, I got it. There's a place, an "invisible box" on the back of a bull, where, if you can stay there, riding one turns from torturous defeat to a total blast! It's all in body positioning. Don't think, "I gotta ride," think about returning to that correct position. When the bull (or in this instance, cow) throws you out of whack, come back to that original position, inside that "invisible box."

I got back on, nodded for the gate, and remember it being so blasted easy that now I was totally embarrassed that I had been falling off so easily before! We never got those heifers to buck out again because suddenly they weren't even a challenge anymore. I could have ridden them blindfolded. I was amazed at how easy it was in comparison to how hard it had felt moments before.

Twenty years have come and gone, and that lesson still speaks to me from time to time. Often, what's hard about life isn't that the circumstances we are facing are so overwhelming; it's that we're out of position. We've allowed ourselves to get sloppy. We've moved from that "place of power" to where the smallest thing whips us around like a rag doll.

There's a place, an "invisible box" that we can literally live from. A lifestyle of going to the Lord Jesus, sitting before Him, asking for His will, His guidance, His wisdom, His strength for the tasks at hand. I have learned not to live <u>for</u> Jesus, but to live <u>FROM</u> Him! The difference is vast. There's a place of strength, a place where you're not the victim anymore; circumstances may not have changed, but the place from which you face them has changed. YOU have changed; you are now positioned for purpose because HIS purposes can now be channeled through you!

When life is getting totally out of hand, check out "where you are," and I'll make a bet…you're out of position somewhere. Make being rightly positioned in Him your priority, and the rest becomes amazingly easier. I'm in no way suggesting all things that come our way are an easy fix! Sometimes what comes doesn't just hurt or inconvenience us, but it can literally <u>destroy</u> us through the pain it brings.

While hurting like hell, we can experience a sense of HOPE in HIM!! The fact is, rightly positioned in Jesus supersedes <u>all</u> that life or death can throw at us!

Keep your position correct, and you WILL be victorious! Guaranteed.

Bull Riding Down Under

A few years back we went to Australia. We had several things to do there, but the main reason was to be a part of twenty years of the ministry of friends in the cowboy world down under. We did many things along the way; we surfed, snorkeled, petted kangaroos, visited an Aboriginal community, and the boys even got to para-sail. But you know what I enjoyed most? I rode a bull. Yep…at fifty years old…I got back on a bull. As a part of the celebration, they had a retirees bull-riding event. THAT was totally unfair because it included guys who were still in their twenties! At any rate, I was told I was entered. My first thought was, "You've GOT to be kidding!" I did the calculation in my lightning fast mind, and it had been seventeen years since I had straddled the back of a bull! But eventually with all the lighthearted festivities, I weakened and said I refused to be part of the draw, but if they PROMISED to pick me out a <u>NICE</u> bull, I would do it. With one accord, they chimed in, "Number 90!" (Aussies are A LOT like Texans…I think maybe they could be described as "Texans on steroids," so you NEVER KNOW if they are taking care of you or…"taking care" of you…if you know what I mean.)

The time of the "great moment" came. Bulls were being loaded in the chutes, bells were clanging, and that old feeling of butterflies in the stomach returned. I borrowed spurs from a twelve-year-old, a vest from a teenager, and a glove from another guy. I'm taking off my wedding ring and find myself praying again that I and everyone else there be covered and protected by the blood of Jesus, that angels would be stationed around about us, and "please, Jesus, just don't let me fall off like a *fat woman!*" You know, I was MORE concerned with that than I was about getting hurt!

I slid down on 90's back, took my wrap, slid up on my rope, and …I was amazed at how <u>good</u> this feels! "Yeah, but…the gate ain't open yet." (I actually thought that.) I nodded for the gate, and he came out just like they promised…a nice jump, kicker. He bucked a wide circle to the right, came back around to the chutes, I pulled the tail of my rope, jumped off, and *almost* landed on my feet. It felt GREAT!! It definitely wasn't the rank pen at the NFR, but it felt as good to me as if Troy Dunn had just made a ninety-point ride.

You know, I feel like this little incident was a gift from God, just for me. A little adrenaline rush under the protective hand of the Lord, a chance to do something utterly pointless and foolish…simply for the adventure of it. God is into adventure. I think He hates boredom more than we do. That's why you're not likely to see Him move mightily in stuffy, dead feeling churches…He's looking for some folks with enough courage to do the "out of the ordinary." Are you a seeker of thrills? Seek the One Who created that "rush." To simply seek thrills has killed a lot of people, but to seek Jesus is to become the expression of who God created you to be. Fear not…He won't stuff you into a plastic image of something you hate. If there ever was an expression of joyous adventure…Jesus is it! Who knows, you may find yourself skydiving at age 60 and Jesus hanging with you all the way down…laughing hilariously!

My bull ride in Australia at fifty years of age. Yee-haw!!

No Throttle, No Power

Heading to Colorado, I couldn't get my two-ton truck to go beyond 55 mph, and I had it on the floor to get that! It struggled up the hills, and it was a looooong, tiresome two days for me to make Colorado from Texas. After making it there, I took my truck to a diesel place. The guy took one look and said, "I don't know how you MADE it here!"

He showed me the part that connected my throttle cable to the engine, and it was literally dangling. NO WONDER I couldn't get any power! My truck wasn't getting the fuel to have the power it needed. He reconnected it to the engine block, and off I drove back to Texas with power.

Back in Texas, I began to notice the throttle cable slipping again, so I had someone adjust it. But as I was driving to the next rodeo, suddenly my foot went to the floor, and NO POWER. The part had broken. Someone welded it for me, and I was back out on the road.

I made it to the next rodeo without a hitch, but then as I was driving to my next event and in the middle of Little Rock, Arkansas, among all the traffic of that city, my foot suddenly went to the floor again, and I had NO POWER. That's a creepy feeling, pulling a big rig with animals through a busy city, and suddenly you're "dead in the water." I immediately started asking for the Lord's help as I was HUNG unless He did something. Suddenly the lane to my right was open, and I shifted lanes and prayed to make an exit before the truck quit rolling. I made an exit and then was praying for a place big enough to pull into. There was an incline (thankfully), so I passed up a couple of businesses and spotted an open parking lot ahead. I was praising God for it as I coasted into the empty, nicely paved lot. After I stopped, I looked to see what I had pulled into… it was a funeral home. The part had broken again, and this time it was done for. A mobile fix-it guy ran the part down and had me back on the road in a couple hours. If it'd been in a small country town, I would've been stuck there for days, but Little Rock had what I needed.

The next morning, I asked the Lord what He was saying in all this, because WHAT happened and WHERE I ended up was just too obviously weird. He said, "No longer can we patch up the old and continue to move forward in power." God is doing a "new thing," and we must shift from old lifestyles and old habits. He spoke very sternly to me that if we continue to simply try to stay in our old ways, we will be without any power to move forward with Him, and we will end up stranded in a place where dead things get buried. This refers to all individuals for sure, but it also refers to people who claim to be believers in Jesus but live according to what's acceptable by the world's standard and not God's. They are going to find themselves in a dangerous position. Also, ministries that are stuck in the rut of old ways and who have a greater loyalty to traditions of man over moving with what God is doing NOW will be left on the side of the road without power, completely out of the flow of God. God isn't playing. To be without power on the highway is dangerous…to be without power in the coming days is DEADLY.

Gunner is always with Colt Wrangler and gets photographed regularly. What can I say? Stardom is such a dog's life!

MISFITS ARE ONLY MISPLACED

Ever feel like a total misfit? Don't ya just hate that feeling? As the saying goes, "About as out of place as a milk bucket under a bull!" Something we need to realize is that "misfits" are only "misfitted." That is, they are out of their element. It has absolutely NOTHING to do with value or worth, just placement.

I once owned a horse we called Bugs. He was born on our place, and I started him from the ground up so he had never been treated wrong. He was smart, very loving, and a super athlete. Problem was, he LOVED having fun, and fun to him was bucking. He didn't have a mean bone in his body; he just loved action! Lots of it. Finally, at eight years old and STILL bucking, I came to the wakeup call that he wasn't going to quit. Oh, he wouldn't buck all the time, but when he did…Yeehaw!!!! You could never afford to go to sleep on him, and though he handled really well, you just never knew when he would un-cork you! I began praying and asking God where this horse belonged. It certainly wasn't with me. How do you sell a horse like that?

"Oh, and by the way, he LOVES to buck…and when he gets the urge, you won't just bounce off…oh no. You'll be DRILLED like a yard dart!"

Oh yeah, folks line up to buy a horse like that!

Everything that God created has a place, and with that place comes purpose. Our quest in life is to find that purpose, and there we will find where we fit. We eventually sold Bugs to a PRCA Stock Contractor who just loved him. He's fat, sassy, and happy (Bugs, not the stock contractor). Flank strap on or off, makes no difference to Bugs…He just LOVES to buck! He loves to see new places, and he likes people. They told me a story of how Bugs bucked off this cowboy pretty hard and fast, turned around and nuzzled him while he was still on the ground, like "Sorry, buddy," and then trotted over to the pickup men like, "Job done." Bugs loves his job!

While to us, Bugs was simply a feed bill and definite disappointment, where he is now, he has great value. Same horse, different placement. Where we fit is where we SHINE.

Trying to throw myself back to center point…
PRCA rodeo Billings, MT 1986

THE VALUE OF THE UNSEEN

There was…as in "used to be"…an old, shot-with-bullet-holes sign on the dirt road river crossing to my house. It had long lost its sturdy stance by time, occasional bumps from trucks, and of course, the floodwaters themselves, and it was leaning heavily. Well, my eyes had fallen upon that old sign, and I was thinking about driving down to the river some night with tools and some WD-40 to "recover" it. One day when driving through the river, I pointed it out to my son and mentioned wanting that old sign.

Upon returning from a five-week road trip, I pulled into my place so glad to be off the road for a while. When I stepped into my bedroom, there on the floor leaning up against the wall was this sign…"LOW WATER CROSSING." I KNEW who had gotten it for me! Or should i say "tactically acquired," as my son in the army likes to call it. It made me smile to know he loved me enough to remember something I had said in passing, and when coming out to my place to pick up something of his, he had the forethought to bring what it took to relieve that old sign of its imprisonment to that shaky old pole. (Have you noticed how I have been cleverly careful to avoid such words as *vandalism*?) I totally look at it as more appropriately considered a RESCUE…yes, that's it!

It wasn't until hours later after finding the sign that I realized Colt had taken a magic marker and written me a message on the back of that old sign. I read it and got teary eyed, for on the backside he had written how he loved me, was so blessed to have me as his mother, and how proud he was of me. WOW!

I loved that old sign anyway, beat up, shot up, somewhat rusted, and dented all over…but NOW I look at it, and guess what I see in that old sign? Yep, you got it. I see the heart of my son's love toward me. I see what's written on the backside of it that no one can see, but I know is there! I see LOVE. I see my son's heart every time I look at that sign. I don't see the dents and blemishes…I see TREASURE.

I think that MUST be how God sees those of us who love Him. He sees past the dents, imperfections, and wounds and sees our HEART. That sign is hanging inside my house, not outside with the other old signs I've acquired over the years. No, this one hangs in a protected environment! Someone could walk into my house and wonder WHY I would have such an old, beat-up sign hanging on my living room wall. They only see the exterior, but I know what's written on the other side that is more precious than the sign itself. I think that's just a very small example of how God sees us when our hearts are completely given over to Him. He sees what's written inside!! The love of a son or daughter who's allowed Him to write upon our hearts...messages of love! You see, when it all boils down, it's not simply the thing we do or are, but the MOTIVE BEHIND who we are and what we do! God looks at what's written inside. Why not make it a "love letter?"

Big Cues, Subtle Cues, and Gigantic Cues

Have you noticed how you train a horse using a series of cues, applying the biggest and easiest to recognize and at the same time, the lighter ones also? As the young horse begins to recognize the cues, you can drop the big ones, and the cues just get lighter and lighter. The lighter the cues, the more sensitive and highly trained the horse. Well, God uses that very same method in teaching His kids how to follow His leads. When we're young in Him, He places bold directives out there for us not to miss! But He has no intention of always having to lead us this way…no more than a horse trainer plans on plow reining his horse forever! So just like horses, as we mature in our walk with the Lord, His directives can become slighter. He…like a good horseman…wants us to become SENSITIVE to His leads. Oh…and He doesn't always talk to us the same way forever. Just as a horseman may shift how he trains because he's teaching a completely different discipline than what he has taught in the past. God speaks through His Word, the Bible. He speaks by a still, small, quiet voice down inside us. He speaks through numbers, colors, movies, songs, a gentle breeze, through our children, our animals…ad infinitum! Why? Because the object isn't simply to learn the "cues"…but to know HIM! He desires our heart, not simply dull obedience. He LOVES simply hanging out with us and enjoying our company! He's not some boss who only wants a good day's work for what he's invested in you, but isn't personally interested in who you are! Believe it or not…He ENJOYS YOU!!

I'm learning to try and go with the flow with how God is interacting with me. In the past, He has communicated with that "unction" on the inside and also DREAMS…lots of dreams! But for the past few years, my dreams have been sparse, and I'm trying to pick up on other ways He's speaking to me.

One thing I have become aware of is that He actually loves to just have FUN with us! I never knew that before quite like I'm realizing it here lately. The other day I was leaving San Antonio in my Freightliner, headed to Wheeler's in Boerne to pick up my trailer. Traffic was rather heavy, and I didn't want to miss my exit, but I wasn't exactly sure which exit it was! No sooner had I finished breathing a prayer for Him to help me not miss the correct exit and already trying to get "sensitive" inwardly so as to not miss His leading than a semi passed me, and on the back it had a life-size picture of George Strait. HELLO…what country girl isn't going to notice THAT!

And in big letters, it said, "Follow me to Wheeler's…Exit 543!!" I laughed out loud!! How much LOUDER could God have said it??!!

Either God thought I was too dull to get it right…OR…He was enjoying His own humor and our relationship!! I don't know about you, but I tend to think it's the latter. Don't misunderstand this and start thinking that God is just our "good buddy" and not to be held in honor and even feared as Scriptures say, but as we mature in our relationship with Him, we discover that He LOVES to play with His children!! What a COOL God He is!!

Playing on the Sabinal River, Utopia, TX

Christmas Surprise

When you're a kid, Christmas is a very special time, full of memories. One particular Christmas stands out in my mind. We had a palomino colt born on the place, and I had fallen in love with him (as little girls often do). Dad's plan was to sell him. He never let on that he was going to change his mind or be swayed in the least.

Christmas came, and my present from Mom and Dad was wrapped up under the tree. Eagerly I tore it open to find a clue written on a piece of paper. Dad said, "This will lead you to your present." I excitedly began running to where this clue led, only to find another clue that led somewhere else. They took me all over, inside, outside—one, I think, was in the oven. At about my fifth or sixth clue, I headed for the barn. There to my utter joy was the palomino colt with a note saying "Merry Christmas" taped to his halter! I could have just cried. Dad got LOTS of hugs and kisses.

You know, that horse has long been gone, but the memory of a father's love is still ever with me. It wasn't only the gift that made it so special, it was the WAY that Dad gave it. He followed me around, not helping in the least, laughing at my childish frustration, getting sheer joy at my ability to finally figure it out, and drinking in my utter excitement as the game was afoot. You know, come to think of it now, I remember those things MORE than I remember the horse! I guess as I've matured, what really matters has changed. Back then, it was the gift that was most important to me. Now, it's the memory of the one who gave it that means so much.

Isn't it like that with our Heavenly Father? He often gives us what we desire, but not by just dumping it in our laps. He gives us His words, written down, that will lead us to our desire, and then walks with us to personally keep tabs on our progress. He laughs at our childish frustrations, gets joy in watching us overcome obstacles, and drinks in our passion for what He gives in life. God is not sitting idly by in His heavenly recliner while we go about life's business; He is ever present with us while the game is afoot. I've noticed something else about my walk with God. As I've matured, I find that I'm not NEAR as interested in what He can give me as I am simply in HIM! I delight to KNOW Him. Each Christmas season may we all not get caught up in the "stuff" and forget that what we are supposed to be celebrating is the greatest gift that God ever gave mankind—HIMSELF! Jesus wasn't wrapped up and placed under a tree but instead, stripped, beaten, and nailed ON one! He was given for the purpose of restoring man's relationship to a loving Heavenly Father. God help us all not to be so interested in what we get out of life, but in finding the One Who GIVES it!

Snubbed Up

We do it with colts. People who show cattle do it with calves.

You know, snubbing something up to something else so the "snubbee" can learn from the "snubber!" We got a heifer to show and got tired of her dragging the boys around the lot, so we took her to a friend's house and snubbed her up to his donkey for three days. The heifer was big and stout, but she had met her match in the donkey. That donkey accomplished in three days what we couldn't get done in three weeks. By the time she got out of "cow purgatory," she had a different attitude entirely!

I saw Tommy Turvey have a blue heeler pup snubbed up to his older, well-behaved blue heeler at a rodeo one time. I thought it was a great idea. Snub up a pup to a well-mannered dog to help train him for you, kinda show him the ropes. Colt Wrangler got a Border collie pup so he could have something to work his 4-H projects. While at a rodeo, Colt snubbed "Johnny Ringo" up to "Huckleberry," our 100+ pound pit bull cross. It worked awesome. Huck would go and Ringo would drag/go for just a bit, but with the size difference, all resistance was gone inside five minutes. When we would stop and visit, Huck patiently waited, so guess what Ringo had to do? Yep…it was working wonders. Huck's sweet attitude and GREAT PATIENCE began to attract much attention, and someone even offered Colt $500 for Huckleberry. Whether they were serious or not, we'll never know because Colt wouldn't consider selling Huck. Don't think I've ever seen a better babysitter. Ringo learned super fast, and in just a little bit, the four-month-old Border collie was sitting and patiently waiting on us while we stood around, keeping his attention on us when we moved.

If we're smart enough to know this works with our animals, why don't we realize the same principle is working on our kids! Know who your kids are snubbed up with! Don't think for one minute that those kids with lower moral standards won't have an effect on yours! The Bible says, "Bad company corrupts." God knew about this snubbing-up thing long ago.

If I tied Ringo to a chicken-killing dog, guess what Ringo would do? Kill chickens. If your kid is running with kids who are drinking, doing drugs, experiencing sex, etc., guess what YOUR kid is going to do?? It doesn't take a rocket scientist's brain to figure that one out. Keep a diligent eye on who your kid hangs with…'cause THAT'S what he's going to become! And by the way, while our kids are snubbed to us, their parents, what are they learning? Are we courteous? Honest? Do <u>we</u> respect authority? Do <u>we</u> keep our word? How do <u>we</u> act when a policeman pulls us over? How do <u>we</u> respond when <u>we</u> lose? Make no mistake, our kids are becoming like who they are around…just as sure as Huck left his mark on Ringo!

The Texas Hill Country offers great motorcycle riding.

Tyger Tuff loves exploring, camping, rock climbing,
and otherwise enjoying the rugged outdoors.

Suffering at Belize…yeah, that's what this is…

A GRAY THING

In the span of three weeks, my gray stallion broke a hind leg, and we had to put him down, then we drove across country to take our oldest son, Tyger, to West Point, where he is to become a part of that "long gray line." One gray gone…another begun.

It's hard to express the feelings I had. Kinda like a huge spoon scooped out a big part of my insides. My beautiful horse, the very best I'd ever owned so far, was gone. Our son, Tyger, was also gone. Gone to become the man God created him to be. Neither will return to me such as they are. Tyger will come home for occasional visits, but the "boy" is forever gone, and a man will return in his place.

Cutting those strings is hard, but they must be cut. Anything that clings is like a leech that sucks out life. If I cling to the memory of a dead horse, I will never invest my heart into another. If I cling to the boy I watched walk away, I will forfeit the ability to relate to the man who will return in his place. Life is a cycle of beginnings and endings. Ride each moment while it is ours to ride and don't waste the next phase while longingly gazing back at what once was. Other horses will come, and if I don't cling to what I lost, I will appreciate what comes my way. As for Tyger? I have cried more since "R day" than I ever expected. It feels to me like a death, and I think I know why. My relationship with my son changed the moment he took the oath and marched away with a newly shaved head. My part in shaping him has changed from a major position to a minor one. I have just passed the baton off to another, and the baton that I passed off is my son.

Though our lives are forever entwined, I must have the courage to accept what he is to become while remembering fondly without clinging to who he used to be. May God grant Tyger as well as the other cadets the courage to be men and women of honor, valor, and integrity. May they become our country's future heroes, and may that long gray line continue on.

Duty, Honor, Country

Tyger Tuff Lyons
West Point
Class of 2011

Speed Bump, my beautiful three-year-old QH stallion,
sired by Patch The Buck one year before breaking his leg.

OF COWS AND MEN

Back in the late seventies, I lived on a ranch in southern Georgia. They had this cow on the ranch that had three horns. Yep—three. The third horn was out of the center of her head. No fooling. There was a growth on the front of her head, like she started to be born with two heads but all that was fully formed was this horn sticking out, kinda like a unicorn. By the time I came to live on this ranch, she was older and meaner than a junkyard dog. When she was younger, they had hauled her around to county fairs and circus shows until she got so mean from all the jeering and picking of the public, they couldn't take a chance on getting her around people anymore. Can't say as I blame her. Everybody has their limits—even cows.

Problem was, now that she was in a safe place, where she belonged, and around people who were there to take care of her, not harass her, she still responded as if we were all her enemies. And buddy, she knew she had three horns, where each of them was, and how to use them! You couldn't get close to her on foot or on horseback without endangering yourself. That third horn made it hard to deal with her. Whenever we drove the pickup out to check the cattle, you could get out and walk among them—all except her. You stayed in the truck around her. She'd come looking for you. Always challenging you. Past injustices had altered her personality to the point that in her mind ALL humans were her enemy.

We can be like this cow. Because of an unfriendly environment, we can come out fighting. We can justify this as a matter of survival, but the problem is, our environment can change—but then we do not. We grow up, we get out of that "hell hole," that abusive marriage, etc., and get connected with people who love us and sincerely care for us, but we can't seem to drop our guard and stop using that extra horn we've developed and know how to use all too well. We know we shouldn't, and we really hate ourselves for responding the way we do, but we can't seem to stop it. Why? Because we have not fully allowed God to deal with our past. Only God can reach down inside us, heal our wounds, and remove our scars. This only comes as we allow God to have total access into our lives and as we make a choice, a deliberate decision, to forgive those who have wronged and wounded us. It doesn't happen totally overnight, but every little bit that we give God access to is just that much more freedom and glorious liberty in our lives. How wonderful it is not to be angry down on the inside! If this, in any way, however small, describes you, I want to encourage you to just ask Jesus to reveal to you anything that needs to be dealt with and removed. Give Him permission to go as deep as your wounds go. He loves you enough to do it and not condemn you for it. Let God turn your tragedies into triumphs! You know, this ranch at one time turned down $10,000 for that cow.

What the world calls a "freak" is often times a very valuable asset to someone who can see its real value. We are like this. Others may have discarded you, used you, and made a sideshow of you, but God saw you of such value to Him that He was willing to pay the ultimate price of His Son, just for the chance to own you for Himself. Don't let others dictate to you your value—you are of priceless worth to the Master!

Oh yeah, and one more thing: drop that dadgum horn!

THE JOURNEY HOME

I was raised in the Ozark Mountains of southern Missouri. Our farm was backed up to thousands of acres of national forest. I grew up roaming those hills on foot and horseback. It was awesome, and I loved it. One fork of the Little Black River ran through the length of our farm. I knew it like the back of my hand, on and off our land. One of my most favorite places to go was a large rock outcropping that was high above the river. It was under a lot of beautiful pine trees, and thick moss covered the ground. You could see the river in both directions for a long ways. I loved it there. I loved the way it felt. I loved its solitude. I loved the way it smelled. I loved all the sounds—the wind through the pines, the sound of water running over rocks, and bull frogs singing. I always found it hard to leave "my special place."

One such evening, I stayed to watch the sun go down over the river. Before I realized, it had grown <u>so</u> dark that I couldn't even see the outline of the hills against the sky. My horse was tied to a tree a safe distance off. I went the way I *thought* he was—no horse. I went another direction. Still no horse. No problem, you can always <u>hear</u> a horse if you just stay quiet long enough. He'll move, stomp his foot, breathe heavy— something. I waited—and waited. <u>Not</u> a sound. I struggled around in the woods for a while longer, getting tangled in vines, falling over rocks, until I came to the realization—I no longer knew where I was. Without being able to see the skyline, I had no idea which direction was north or south, which direction I had fumbled around to, and most importantly, which direction was <u>home</u>. As I stood there wondering how to get out of the mess I had gotten myself into, I became aware of that wonderful, ever-so-faithful sound of the river. I knew the river would take me home, so I made my way down the hillside toward it. I hoped I could walk along the river's edge, but the thick brush, dense rocks, and saw briers were nigh impenetrable. I had no choice but to get into the river and wade it home. It was only a couple of miles to the house, and I knew there were no holes of water deeper than chest deep, so I started home, praying that God would keep me safe from the cottonmouth snakes. It was hard walking, and the water was <u>cold</u>. By the time I got home, I was <u>exhausted</u>, chilled to the bone, and looked an absolute fright, but happy as a pig in a mud hole to be <u>home</u>!

Mom and Dad embraced me, got me dried off and into warm clothes, questioned me, and even commended me for using my head. Then Dad handed me a flashlight and said, "Now go get your horse."

"You mean, <u>walk</u> back? Aren't you going to take me on the tractor or something?"

He explained that it was my irresponsibility that had gotten me *into* this jam in the first place, and I had to learn the consequences of my actions. It was a l-o-n-g walk back, a grateful ride home, and I don't remember a warm bed ever being more welcome! I never did it again.

Our Heavenly Father is like this. When we've "played out in the woods" too long, gotten ourselves into a desperate situation and then turned for "home" willing to do <u>whatever it takes to get there</u>—the Father is always waiting to embrace us, comfort us, take care of our immediate needs, and then "fix" us. And *always* in the fixing of us, He will demand of us to take responsibility for our actions. *Sometimes*, He will even require us to go back to where we've come from and make things right. Oh, and one other thing. The way "home" is <u>God's</u> way. Often, the only way back is the *last* way <u>we</u> would choose! God's way is like a river that flows back to Him. Playing along the riverbank will not get you there and will only get you beat up. There's only one way—take the plunge—get into the river and let Jesus lead you. Salvation isn't always easy—but it's <u>great to be home</u>!

My mom and dad, Paul and Juanita Mangold, always going
on adventures during the eight years they lived in Alaska.

A Close Encounter of the Most "Unforgettable" Kind

When I was a kid back in the hills of Missouri, we used to have open range. Folks just branded their cattle and notched their hogs' ears and let 'em roam free. There were plenty of woods, water, grass, and acorns to go around. We had some pretty "salty" lookin' hogs. They had to be. Nicer bred hogs that were more domestic let too many coyotes steal their piglets. I'll never forget this one sow; her name was Ole Crow. She came by that name honest. She could clear any normal fence. It was a sight to behold; she could jump it like a deer. She got into our cornfield—more than once. Got ran out of our cornfield with buckshot—more than once. I remember Dad saying that if she wasn't such a good momma, he'd have sold her long ago. She never lost a piglet. But ugly… she was ugly! She had that old razorback look to her, and I'll *never forget*—she had light-colored eyes. Very intimidating, *mean-looking*, light-colored eyes.

One day, Dad had all the hogs rounded up and penned at the barn so that he could notch ears and clip tushes. I *badly* wanted to be there. I was about five or six at the time. Dad told me to get up in the hayloft right above where he was working and *stay put*. I had a great view to watch from there. Was I satisfied? Nooooo! I wanted to help! Dad was busy clipping tushes, baby pigs were squealing, and sows were outside Dad's working pen, making that "woofing" noise that hogs make when they're upset. Unbeknownst to Dad, I slipped out of the hayloft and was out in the barnyard making my way around to the back of the barn where all the "action" was.

Before I got very far, here came Ole Crow—heading straight for me. I panicked—which was a very reasonable thing to do, considering the situation. There was a large pile of lumber nearby. I ran up that pile. Like sure that's going to save me?! She clears fences! Ole Crow ran up the pile after me. I was screaming, but Dad couldn't hear me over the squealing of the pigs. There was nothing else to do but run for Dad as fast as my little legs could carry me! Crow was right on my rear, "woofing" all the way, and I am *convinced* that if I would have tripped and fell, she would have killed me right then and there. I was running as fast as I could, yelling "Daddy!" hard as I could every step of the way! Dad saw us, grabbed up a board, and headed toward me. I made it to Dad, and Ole Crow didn't get me. (I guess you've done figured that part out since I'm here writing this.) I jumped up in his arms and kept climbing 'til I was perched on his shoulders. I was so *scared* that I peed all over Dad! I don't think he even cared at the moment; he was too busy beating Ole Crow off of both of us! I had learned my lesson. I was <u>totally</u> satisfied to stay within those set boundaries after that!

God, as our Heavenly Father, has set boundaries for us to live by.

Those boundaries are oftentimes looked upon as being there just to take our freedom and fun away, but that's a misconception. God's boundaries are there for our life, health, peace, and safety. But just like I did back then, most of us got to slip across the line some time or another in an attempt to get our way! Sometimes we can find ourselves in a worse situation than having an angry hog on our butt! What's the answer? Same. Run to the Father, calling on the Name of Jesus! He'll save you. Don't worry about cleaning yourself up before you come. You don't have time, and furthermore, you <u>can't</u>! It ain't about looking pretty. It's about being safe! Just like my daddy didn't throw me aside because I peed all over him, neither will Jesus cast you aside—in *all* your mess! He doesn't care what you look like or where you've been— He just cares about <u>you</u>!

THE DOOR

Some doors are very pleasant to walk through, others—well, I need to just tell you the story. We were at the coliseum in Abilene for the Texas High School Rodeo Finals. It was late, and we were waiting for the rodeo to be over to do the Wednesday night cowboy church service we all lovingly called "midnight mass." I was dog tired and decided to head for the bathroom to be ready for the service. I was kinda extra in the "mully-grubbs" because I had been asking God all day to let me know what He wanted me to minister that night, and so far had heard nothing. I was lollygagging along, not even looking up as I opened the door to the ladies' bathroom. Bummed out because of not hearing anything from God, I didn't bother to look up—I'd been here too many times. I knew where everything was like the back of my hand.

Still looking down to let my dog come in with me, I bumped into the largest lady I've ever bumped into. Strangely enough, my face was bumped up against a very stiffly starched brushpopper shirt, and I was looking down at the biggest pair of boots I'd ever seen on a woman. My lightning-fast mind began to calculate all the information. Women don't usually stand six-feet-plus tall and feel like you've bumped into a rock when you come up to them. Not to mention the size of this one's feet, and the fact that women don't usually wear stiffly starched brush popper shirts—I'm wide awake by this time.

I quickly decided it wouldn't be wise to look around, so I just brought my gaze from looking at those huge boots skyward to just below the brim of a black cowboy hat. A very tall, very broad-shouldered cowboy was standing quietly before me, grinning like a traveling rat. I then asked the question of all questions—"Am I in the men's bathroom?" (Why is it that when we are already hung out to dry, we make matters worse by blurting out something extra ordinarily stupid?)

He simply replied, "Believe so." Right then I let out a scream and slapped the poor guy on the arm (don't have a clue as to why I did that either).

He said, "What ya hittin' me for? I ain't in your bathroom—you're in mine!"

I turned and ran out the door straight into a crowd of people gathered around, all laughing, slapping one another, and grinning like egg-sucking dogs. They had seen me going into the men's bathroom, and instead of stopping me, they all began hollering at friends to come and watch the festivities. Texans are ornery that way!

Ever heard the statement, "all roads lead to heaven?" What an utterly stupid thing to say! Yeah, right—all roads lead to heaven like all doors lead to the women's bathroom! Come on, get real! We don't hang our brains out to dry like that in anything else other than spiritual matters. Believing all roads lead to heaven is like believing all roads lead to Cheyenne, Wyoming! That kind of "non-thinking" will get you lost as a goose in a snowstorm! Jesus Himself said, "I am the way, the truth and the life, no man comes to the Father except by Me." (John 14:6) Jesus also called Himself "the door" in John 10:9. That "the" part means there is no other—He's it! When I missed the right door at the rodeo, it only cost me embarrassment, but to miss the right door in life will cost you eternity! Miss Him—and you've missed it all.

Well, I suddenly had the ministry material and leading that I needed for that night's service! Come to think of it, the attendance was real good, and there was a lightheartedness among the people—a good time was had by all. It's amazing what one wrong door will do!

Fear: Conquer It or It Will Conquer You!

Fear is something that everyone must deal with. We either face it or run from it. I have found a couple of principles that minimize the "fear factor" greatly. One of which is "know you are in the will of God."

When I <u>know</u> that I am obeying God to the best of my ability, my life has been given into His hands, and my desire is to be yielded and obedient to Him, I have great confidence—no matter what the situation looks like. People living outside of God's will do not have that kind of confidence.

One time when I was flying, we were in some pretty rough turbulence for a while, and the lady sitting next to me was beginning to freak. I quietly told her not to be afraid because nothing was going to happen to this plane. She asked how I could be so confident. I told her I knew it because I was in God's will; where I was supposed to be at this time, and my call in life, was not yet finished, so NOTHING was gonna happen to this plane.

She said, "I sure hope so."

Two people in the same situation—one in total peace (though nauseated) and the other tormented by fear—simply because one was in God's will and one was not.

Years ago when I was riding rough stock, I was entered in the girl's bareback bronc riding at a PRCA rodeo in Los Angeles. It had taken almost all my money just to get there and pay my fees, and I bucked off my first horse. I had only $20 and one more horse to get on. They were big, stout horses, and if I didn't win something, I was stuck in Los Angeles. The "pucker factor" was getting pretty intense.

Right then I "heard" the Lord say, "Didn't I call you to do this?"

Yes, Lord.

"Then I'll take care of you. Get your eyes off yourself, and get your focus back on Me."

I repented and peace returned in the midst of fear. Can you understand that?

My next horse was a bucker! It was the best ride I ever made! The crowd went wild, and I won that go-round and placed well in the average. My confidence had shifted from me to Him. The difference it makes is phenomenal.

The other principle is this: When God is telling you to do something and you are afraid, *do* it afraid! When it is the will of God, <u>face</u> fear, and you will conquer it. Run from fear, and it will conquer you! I have found that whenever I face something while I am afraid, fear loses its power over me. Give into it just a little in one area of life, and it will begin taking over other areas! Fear is a tyrant. It seeks to rule and dominate. It's kinda like terrorism, dominate it or it will dominate you. There is no neutral ground when dealing with fear!

Winning the go-round on this bucker!
Flying U PRCA Rodeo, Los Angeles, CA 1987

Whatever Happened to the Woodshed?

My first grade in school was spent in the last one-room schoolhouse still in operation in the state of Missouri. It was GREAT. I would walk, or ride my Shetland pony the mile and a half through the woods to school and leave him in a barnyard all that day, then ride him home again. My memories of that time are very colorful, vivid, and sweet. There were two outhouses, one on each side of the schoolyard; one for boys and one for girls. A potbellied wood stove stood in the middle of the room, and a big wooden kitchen table covered in books served as our library.

Then there was the woodshed. It served a dual purpose. It held the stockpile of wood for the stove and also provided the place where, on occasion, a student was taken to be out of "earshot" (almost) for the purpose of "intensive attitude adjustments." I shall never forget one of those days.

Their names were Daine and Wayne. They were identical twins. So much so that only a couple of students could tell them apart. I was not one who could, and neither was the teacher. Both boys were in their last year at Lone Star School, the eighth grade. They were big, stout boys that were tough and used to working hard in the log woods. Anyway, for whatever reason, one of the boys hit a kid in the schoolyard. Problem was, the kid that got belted couldn't tell them apart and went crying to the teacher, nursing a very bloody nose. She immediately called both boys in for questioning. Wayne swore that Daine did it, and Daine said Wayne did it. They were confident that they had the teacher stumped. She never faltered for a second. After giving them time to come clean and seeing it wasn't going to happen, she promptly took them BOTH to the woodshed. The whole school was "lopsided" as we all ran to the woodshed side of the schoolhouse, with our faces stuck to the windows. Though they were the size of grown men, in no time at all, we could hear them squalling like a mashed cat. Instant order was again regained.

It's amazing how quiet it gets and how much work you can get done just after something like that kinda sets the standard, and all nerve to challenge that standard has departed.

Times have changed, and that old schoolhouse isn't there anymore. We've changed as well…possibly more so than the times. Now, instead of a whipping (or whooping, where I came from), we have time-out. Oh yeah. That strikes fear into the heart of the rebellious! If that doesn't work, we give it a name and prescribe a drug, thus telling society (as well as the child) that they can't help being obnoxious… thus, we must just learn to put up with their bad manners and lack of respect for authority. It's not their fault! We now have "call letters" for these "disorders": ADD, ADHD, (and a new one I heard the other day that I especially like), ADLBD. (attention-deficit, lazy butt disorder)! I realize that sometimes there are physical problems that a child is dealing with. But for the most part, what I've personally witnessed is more the results of parents who don't spend the time, and consistency it takes, to discipline their children and get a handle on them at an early age. They want to reason with a two-year-old and then suddenly lay the law down when the kid is ten or twelve! It's backward…and too late.

Anyone with an IQ above room temperature would know you can't take a horse ten or twelve years old that's never been disciplined, saddle it up, and expect to suddenly bring it under the same strict disciplines that have taken years of consistent training to get in other horses. Same with children. Manners aren't born in us; they're developed through discipline early on. Round pens can be purchased easily for training colts…but whatever happened to the woodsheds?

Lone Star School, the last one-room schoolhouse
in Missouri. Notice the outhouse in the background.
That's me in the front, far left, looking "extra cool"
in my bright red dime-store cowboy hat.

Cut Off by a Cross Fence

I like to walk while I pray. The dirt road that goes by my house drops down to a little wet weather creek and then continues up a very tall hill that has a magnificent view of the hill country. I like walking up that hill. The dogs are always with me, and this particular morning, Zeke found an opening in the fence at the creek bottom and darted under the fence to enjoy a cool dip in the water. I kept walking, the older dog staying right by my side. Zeke came splashing out of the water hole, but instead of going back through the hole in the fence to get back on the road, he just headed up the fence line. Well…you know, that ain't gonna fly for long, but he don't know that. The fences on this place are excellent…goatproof quality. Zeke doesn't know it, but unless he goes back to that spot where he got behind the fence, he's NOT going to be able to continue walking with me.

But of course, happy as a lark with tongue hanging out, he continues to travel parallel with me up the hill…until he came to a cross fence. I kept walking, and he was cut off from continuing on with me. Oh, the barking and howling! But no amount of vocalizing his distress was going to make that cross fence go away! I kept walking and praying while listening to his complaints till I reached the crest of the hill and turned to walk back down. Once Zeke made it through the fence to be reunited with me and Huck, he was one happy camper!

I really didn't think anything about this until later on that day when God used that little incident to talk to me personally. That was an accurate depiction of where I've been lately…. behind a fence with God…able to see Him but not close enough to be touched by Him. Thinking that I was still walking with Him but somehow feeling a distance growing between us. He let me know that we can allow pain to come between us and Him. It's while in the valley that we can be enticed to <u>linger</u> a little too long in our pain and sorrows, and unbeknownst to us, we have allowed that pain, sorrow, hurt, betrayal, etc., to become a barrier between us and Him. We're still following the Lord…just not as close as we used to. We have allowed a justified emotion to take an unjustified place in our lives. HE should be what we are drawn to…not some wallowing hole of self-pity. But we go there…all of us do from time to time. I just didn't realize how dangerous it is to my relationship with the Lord. I kept myself from feeling His touch by embracing a negative emotion while I "barked and complained" over the barrier between us…a barrier of my own making. He didn't respond to my loud protests any more than I did to Zeke's. Zeke must learn to stay WITH me…any distance has its price…a lesson that God wants me to learn as well.

There has to be a time when we cannot be enticed away from the manifest presence of our Lord by ANYTHING…highs or lows. Emotions are God's gift to us; they are to be like spice…adding flavor and zest to life…or bringing depth to our soul…but they were never intended to rule. If we allow emotions to rule the day, we are well on our way to being separated from the very life flow of God.

Tyger speaking at a 4-H Awards Banquet

CATCHING WILD CATTLE

Many moons ago…MANY moons, we had dogs specifically for catching wild cattle. It was a total blast to do…rough…and the pay was bad, but it was FUN! Most times when we got called to go catch something, it was on a river bottom, where it was simply too overgrown to pitch a loop on one. You had to have good dogs to get the job done.

We had Catahoula dogs for tracking and baying and pit bulls for catching. Most of our pits were long legged and capable of keeping up and still having the energy it took to catch and hold one, but I remember this one female pit we got that was very short and stout. We actually had a tarp that was sown to fit over the saddle horn with four pockets to put her legs down in, so she could brace herself and ride 'til we got the cow bayed and ready to catch. We hadn't had her long, and she was new to the game, but this "ride 'til we get there" seemed like a good idea at the time. The Catahoulas had the cow bayed in a swamp, and we were almost there when the pit simply couldn't stand it any longer. She could hear the dogs in a frenzy and was SO EAGER to get into the game. Not being able to stand it anymore, she reached down and grabbed the neck of the horse. Poor horse…he swallowed his head. Poor cowboy…he had ropes, pit bull, brush to contend with…and now a horse that thought it had been caught by a mountain lion! I remember stuff flying in every direction…ropes, reins, dog, cowboy. It was one of those unforgettable wrecks.

When it was over and all involved was found to be just fine, we laughed 'til we hurt…rehashing every action and expression with animated gestures. You know the commercial…horse: $5,000…dog: $300…rope: $35…paycheck: lacking…stories to tell: PRICELESS.

I find that we are too often just like this young pit. We have the talent and the ability for something, but our over-anxiousness can get us sidetracked and even delay what we are called to do. Waiting on the right timing is HARD. Whether it's desiring a new job or simply giving a word of correction…timing is EVERYTHING. Look at Moses…he was called, educated, and in a good position to be the deliverer of Israel, but like the pit bull…he didn't wait to be released. He moved on initiative born of impatience and killed a man. That little incident cost Israel another forty years of slavery. An entire generation lived and died slaves as a result of Moses getting ahead of God—trying to do what he was born to do without waiting to be commissioned and empowered by the One Who had called him.

Busted!! I'm soooo guilty of this. I get tired of waiting. I feel like the game is going to be OVER before I ever get a chance to bat! Know what I mean? I grab the neck of the "horse" and then wonder why I'm in a wreck! Waiting is HARD! But if we are going to be effective, we must learn to WAIT until God has things in right order. Waiting is a hard part of life. We are expected to wait 'til supper is cooked…wait to get married…wait 'til we finish our schooling…wait 'til we have the money to buy something…. wait on God to commission us before we step into our calling. *Wait*…it's definitely a four-letter word, but doing it God's way will sure keep us out of a lot of wrecks!

A BREAK FROM BOREDOM

Friends of mine worked a 5,000-acre ranch in the Texas hill country. It's an awesome ranch, with a 23-acre lake and a year-round creek running through. Several of us loaded the horses and trailered them to meet Bob and Amy and go riding. It was a HOT Sunday afternoon, and truly what drove us to ride on such a noncompliant day was simply sheer boredom of sitting under the air conditioner and a longing to see our good friends.

We were saddled up and ready to go at approximately the hottest part of the afternoon. Bob kept saying, "I take pains to NEVER be out riding this time of day," but off we went just the same with a wet bandana tied around Amy's neck, a .22 pistol with rat shot on my hip in case we saw a rattler, and a .38 on Bob's for the wild hogs.

Once we got to the lake, the horses and dogs all hit the water for the sheer comfort of it. After that, it seemed, horses began to feel much friskier. Once we rode to the deep hole in the river with a rope swing, the urge for cooling off had overwhelmed us as well. Next thing you know, Colt Wrangler had peeled down to his blue jeans and was swinging out over the water. That deep "ploosh" sound can be simply irresistible. Before you knew it, pistols, boots, belts, cell phones and such were in piles everywhere as we were dropping into the deep, cool water and enjoying being like kids again.

It was great how wonderfully cool we felt for the duration of the ride with the slight breeze blowing on our wet clothes. After that, things seemed to heighten some. I don't know, something was just in the air. Horses started pitching, then we brushed up several wild hogs. That was the moment we lost sight of Colt's pit bull. Off he went across a creek and disappeared in the rugged terrain. Immediately we heard the high-pitched squeal of a hog. I was on a big colt, so Bob took the lead for me as we hurriedly baled down a bank, across a little creek, and into the brush. In thirty seconds or less, the hog suddenly silenced, but I had my own troubles. My colt started bucking, and can I say I was SO

THANKFUL for the deep sand we were in at the time. Not because of a softer place to land (though that was a consideration), but because I didn't get the full brunt of what he could have dished out. I made it through that storm…I'm sure by the grace of God…and soon after, Bob found Huck heaving from the heat, standing beside his trophy…a very dead hog. Once we caught our breath, I realized my sunglasses were off my head and my pistol had been bucked out of its holster; Colt realized his spur was missing off a boot after his part in the adventure. We prayed, backtracked, and recovered all.

Sometimes that's just what you gotta do; once you make it through a "storm," pray…back track to see where you lost something… and by God's grace, sometimes you can recover all. More important than the "things" we can lose during an adventure is the fear that can keep us from ever having one. God delights in bringing us to a place of recovery as well as giving us a refreshing break from the monotony of "same ole, same ole."

It was a good day all around…good laughs, good times, good friends, and God's grace over it all.

A picture is worth a thousand words they say...

Can Colt Wrangler not just RIDE like everybody else?!!

RIDING OUT STORMS

Ever been in a storm? Sure you have. Chances are, more than one. There are many different kinds of storms. Those of weather, those related to riding or roping, and the storms of life that come our way… sickness, death, divorce, financial disasters, etc. Bet you been in a few, huh? When you're in one, sometimes you wonder if you're going to come out of it alive. Those that we come out of unscathed often make us look back and have a good laugh. Sometimes we come out of those with a cocky attitude…like we were so good to pull that off!

I remember taking a big two-year-old horse to a friend's house to mess around in the arena while they roped. After a while I decided to get him in the heeler box and just lope him out and let him start tracking, while my friend was coming out of the header box to simply rope the steer's horns and follow him down the pen. I placed my boy at the mouth of the box so as to EASE him out there GENTLY. (He's clueless as to what's about to happen…so am I for that matter.) Header nods…chute snaps open…steer runs out…header runs out…we lope out. The whistling of the rope so close to my youngster was a trifle too much. His left ear did that queer flattened-out pointy thing, and I thought, "Oh, dang."

Yep…it ended up being an "oh dang moment." My colt sucked under himself at about two strides out, and that was the last I saw of his head for a bit. Thank God he did that wild, western, "all fours off the ground at the same time" kind of bucking. That's always been easier for me than the "kick over their heads while they travel down the pen" kind of bucking. Less jerk, you know. It's the kind of bucking that, if you stay astride, makes you look cool. Oh yeah…my kind. Anyway…to end this story…ten seconds or so later, all was under control. I was intact… the horse was less afraid of being attacked by a rogue rope…everyone had a good laugh…and I had a rather "safe" adrenaline rush. (Good for folks my age.) The "storm" was over, and I was still on top. Cool. I like those endings.

Ever been in a relationship storm? Those aren't so fun. Usually it's not a matter of coming out on top as it is just coming out…surviving. When you're in something like that…or going through a terrible ordeal such as a health issue, etc., you just want to know if there's even a way out! Dark times.

You may be in a storm of some sort right now. You could be wondering at this very moment if you're even going to make it through this one. I know the feeling. It ain't fun. I have learned that when I'm in a storm like that, I have no option but to trust God and listen (maybe more sensitively) for His voice. Sometimes I hear things I don't like… things that point out my own faults, etc. The toughest times are when I don't hear Him at all. That's when you just gotta "gut it out" and trust His character. He will never leave you nor forsake you. He has a plan…a good plan…for <u>you</u>. Can you trust Him enough to walk through this dark time and not understand? Trusting God; it's kinda like trying to keep your seat in the middle while your body weight is getting pulled this way and that. It's a constant struggle to trust God when you're in the storm and can't see a horizon. But if you are going to come out stronger…better… wiser…you have no choice but to yield yourself to God and trust His will for you in this situation. It's tough I know…but it's God's way. Quiet yourself down and take time to listen. This storm <u>will</u> pass…you'll look back and see the faithfulness of God, and it'll all be worth it.

CHARACTER OR SIMPLY WELL TRAINED?

I once had a visit with a very well-known horse trainer/clinician who had a very WELL-TRAINED horse that he had doing things above and beyond what most horses ever learn to do on cue. As we hung around and talked, he began to tell me how that he would not keep this horse simply because he couldn't be trusted. I was amazed because the horse looked and acted as if he was incredibly yielded and submissive. "Oh, he's well trained and smart," he said, but he continued to tell me that no matter how advanced his training had become, he never could trust him to simply not kick someone at any given moment. He had to watch him like a hawk! He said he figured as time and training went on, that the mean, aggressive streak in this horse would diminish, but it hadn't. Proof that you can have one well-trained horse, but that doesn't mean their character is changed. As I watched this horse, I mistakenly confused being well-trained with having a trustworthy character... the two are by no means the same! We often judge people the same way. We mistakenly attribute good manners to good character...good personality as being a good person. The two are NOT even remotely the same! Think about it...good cons could NEVER be good at what they do unless they came across as a good, trustworthy individual! Just like that horse, we can be duped into thinking a person has good character simply because they have a pleasing personality and well-developed manners. Herein lies the danger. Besides a person's looks, personality is the drawing card. When we fall for an individual, what we are attracted to is their mannerisms and their personality. And if we don't look deeper, we assume that we are seeing their character. We are not! We are seeing their personality, which is theirs naturally, and also their manners which come through training. But CHARACTER IS DEEPER! Character isn't discovered until you watch how that person responds in pressure situations. Before you can know what they are REALLY like, you must observe them through incidents where they are NOT getting what they want, when things AREN'T working in their favor. You have to watch the "little things." It's often the little things that give us a true indication of what's REALLY hidden under the surface. Just as a horse may not kick, but as someone moves around him, his eyes and ears show an inner aggressive attitude and irritable nature…BINGO, you just saw what he's really like! He may be well trained and well guarded, but his eyes and ears didn't lie…they showed the REAL thoughts inside his head. Given time and the right circumstances, what's there is going to come out!

We tend to be so impressed with personality and good manners that we can even dupe ourselves into thinking we are "Good Joes" because we are well mannered…all the while neglecting to look into a more accurate reflection of who we really are deep down. Good character doesn't come easy. It has to be developed slowly over time, and the ONLY way it's developed is by us doing the RIGHT THING even when it COSTS. Be honest, even when it hurts. Giving of yourself even when surrounded by selfishness. Putting out that extra effort even when no one sees or even notices. Good manners can be learned but good character? It COSTS!! When dealing with horses AND people, it pays to look deeper than trained mannerisms. Watch for signs that reveal their REAL character!

Stud Finder

You hear it among single women, you see it in magazines, and you can't even pull up e-mails or Facebook without advertisements about finding the "man of your dreams." Oh pleeeeze!! There's an ad that comes up all the time when I'm checking my e-mails. It says, "Faithful men looking for women."

HELLO! Since when did men EVER need help in finding women?!! And how do we know they're faithful? They filled out a questionnaire and said so? If we fall for this stuff, we seriously need our head examined. Soooo, I've found a simple solution to the problem of finding that "stud" who is upright, stable, positioned well, trustworthy…solid. I did so by accident. I kept poking holes in things, looking in vain, when lo and behold, a small investment solved my dilemma!

I stumbled onto it one day, and it has solved so many problems and taken the hassle out of looking for that stability that you need to secure things on. I invested in a Stud Finder. Yep…$19.95 and your problems are solved! This little gadget lights up and blinks when you are nearing one and then gives a clear tone once you have found it solidly. What else could a girl want? I can now…within minutes…find that stud that stands upright, solid, and strong on which to secure whatever it is that needs securing! Why didn't I think of this before now? It would have saved me years of poking around in the wrong places, looking for something that wasn't even there! This is how it works…next time you feel the need to find that man of your dreams, just stick the Stud Finder in your purse and take it to wherever you are going. Once you get there and single men are standing around, thick as fleas on a dog, just pull out your little Stud Finder and hold it up close to the guy. If it doesn't give you that good, solid sound to indicate a well-placed stud…move on, girl… move on!! I'm telling ya, THIS could revolutionize the dating scene! No more guesswork. There's also a secondary positive to the deal…guys will tend to withdraw from a woman who has the equipment that takes the guesswork out of the scenario. Go figure. All those guys that you held the Stud Finder up to and it signaled you with that "it's not here" sound? They will LEAVE YOU ALONE! Mission accomplished! You may not have found your "stud," but you warded off all the ones who aren't it!

I'm serious. Girls…ACE Hardware, $19.95…problem solved. There IS one other option we could discuss, but seriously, it's MUCH harder. Every single person could simply seek after the Lord with their entire being and keep themselves pure until HE assures you that this one before you is THE one, get married, and THEN enjoy the benefits of a love relationship based upon a righteous foundation. But if you don't want to pay that kind of a price for a future relationship that will last, you can always fall back on the Stud Finder! Quick-fix gadgets…don't ya just LOVE 'em?!

Christmas at our house! We're a TEXAS family y'all!

My kitchen
always ends
up looking
like this over
the holidays.

Okay…so my son's enthusiasm kinda wears off on ya!

PERCEPTIONS

I heard someone make this observation: "perception is reality to the one perceiving." Meaning, how we perceive is OUR reality. It may or may not be truth, but if we PERCEIVE it to be truth, that perception becomes a reality in our life.

We've all experienced horses that "see" imaginary boogers. You're riding along at a nice, smooth canter, and suddenly you get dashboarded as they shove both front feet into the ground and then dart off to one side or the other. Nothing was there…a shadow…a rock…something moving in the wind…but the horse perceived it to be a monster of some sort and responded in like fashion to their perception. OR…say a barrel horse has some sort of pain that occurs when they set themselves to turn a barrel. You find the problem and fix it…no more pain. But NOW the problem is the horse THINKS it's gonna hurt when they turn that barrel. The REAL danger is gone, but the PERCEIVED danger is still there. Simply correcting the issue isn't enough; you have to also correct the horse's perception of the issue.

You know what I'm going to say next, don't you? WE are the same way. Our perception is our reality, whether it is true or not. Therefore, it's EXTREMELY important that we keep ourselves healed and well on the INSIDE. If I am carrying an unhealed wound from a past hurt, anytime something triggers a familiarity to that incident, I will immediately respond accordingly. Just like that horse that leaps off to the side over a shadow, my response will be to overreact. Why? That incident of pain is long gone, but the inner wound and fear of like pain is still very present. Everyone around is like, "Whoa"…as they stare in disbelief at the way someone just flipped out over nothing. What was that all about? It was simply their perception based upon past hurts. It's not good enough to just "move on"…changing our outer circumstances. We also must allow God to reach down on the inside of us and restore us inwardly.

Everyone has been betrayed, everyone has been cheated…made a fool of…and been done wrong in some form or another. NOW are we going to allow that hurt to be healed so we can learn from it…move on… and be able to trust again, or are we going to simply live a life of never letting our guard down…never allowing anyone to ever get that close ever again? The choice is ours. But know this, our perception IS our reality. If my perception is distorted, my life will be distorted also. I've seen people NOT trust an honest individual, while embracing another who was simply out to get what they could for their own benefit. How could they not see the reality that was so evident in front of everyone's eyes but their own? Their past hurts and selfish fears, etc., made them prime targets for a con. How do we see through the distortions to recognize reality? One way…by allowing the One Who sees and knows all to have full and complete access into the depths of our inner man. No lies…no pretenses…no guilt…no unhealed wounds…no selfish agendas. Just let God's Word in our lives be the final authority. Do what He says. Let Him direct our affairs. He will heal. He will restore. He will lead us into the company of those who are like minded. His perceptions can become ours…and His are ALWAYS accurate!

Show or Go?

I once owned a horse that had been used for multiple speed events until he was soured to the point of not being able to bring him near an arena with his brain intact. I rescued him of sorts…I took him far away from arenas and used him simply to ride pastures on a daily basis, checking cattle. I loved this horse, even though he had a head that favored a moose…so I named him Bullwinkle. Bullwinkle turned out to be a really cool ranch horse, and I actually liked the way he would quickly be on the muscle.

One evening after working cattle with other riders, we were heading back to headquarters, and I was riding alongside an older bay stallion. The stud was a son of Leo; he was a big-boned horse that could work all day in heat or deep snow. He had been run on brush tracks in his younger days and had won twelve out of his thirteen races. Bullwinkle was getting on the muscle, and the Leo horse was walking along with head down and bottom lip hanging. I smarted off and asked if he wanted to race. The reply was a slight grin with the info that I'd be beaten badly. I laughed and said that my horse would be at the finish line before the old guy even knew there was a race happening! You know…smack talk. Well, as we kept battering back and forth while still walking along…I say that loosely…my horse was getting higher by the minute, while the old Leo stallion hadn't even tightened his bottom lip. We decided on a finish line up ahead; while still walking/ bouncing, side by side we counted down to "go." That old Leo horse went from half asleep to full bore in one bat of an eye! My horse was fast…way faster than most horses. We had won a lot of pasture races, but we didn't even come close to winning this one. I never saw the finish line because my vision was only the butt of the big bay from the very first jump!

You could have blown me over with a feather! I never saw anything like it. My horse was ANTICIPATING a race…the old racehorse looked like he was half asleep. How he went from lip dragging to full speed, I don't know, but he did it. I had such respect for that horse from then on, and I didn't put quite as much stock in all the slick, showboat speedy stuff after that old horse spanked my butt and taught me a lesson while doing it.

It's not the mouthy ones who get the job done. The dog to watch isn't necessarily the one barking…the really bad ones don't make noise. The horse to beat isn't always the showy one. Youth doesn't usually win over battle-aged experience. Mouthy braggarts are not usually the ones who can actually DO what they say. Show me a guy dressed like a cowboy with a mouth and swagger bigger than this hat, and I'll bet money he can't sit a horse as well as he does a bar stool!

We put so much stock in show…finery…the ability to speak well and look the part. America has almost lost the ability to see character and integrity over Hollywood show. What charms us is usually not what can hold the line when the battle is raging. Not only do I pray for Americans to again honor the honorable, but I also desire to BECOME a person of honor and integrity, a person of character who's been forged in the former fires and has been found to remain true and trustworthy when the heat is on.

Singing on Strider
INSIDE Solid
Rock Church,
Monroe, OH 2016

A Matter of Trust

The young bull dog I have is suddenly exhibiting such fear of me. I'm taking it quite personally and it's actually hurting my feelings.

To his credit, I didn't start him like other pups I've had. I got him as a playmate for a baby coon. They slept together, played together, tore up anything they could…together. Well, now the coon isn't here and an older dog we had isn't here either. Suddenly it's just me and Zeke, and I'm realizing that we don't have the relationship I thought we had.

I tried to bathe him and he ran off and stayed hid for most of the day. On one of our trips to the river, I shot a snake and Zeke ran away from me as if he was next! We've shot guns at the house before, but I guess he had the older dog as a stabilizer and now that the other dog is gone, he's freaking out. I have come to the sad discovery that what I thought was a trust in me was simply a trust in the things around him. Once removed, it's painfully obvious that this dog doesn't trust me. There is NO relationship without trust. I never really thought very deeply about how trust is such an major thread in the fabric of relationships. I have known that once my trust has been betrayed, I can't seem to give myself unreservedly to that relationship anytime quickly. Trust has to be rebuilt, and if it isn't, the relationship is stalemated to a surface existence at best. That's why a betrayal in a marriage can be forgiven by the wounded partner, but the relationship will suffer deep consequences for years to come and possibly never regain what it once was. Trust has been broken. Forgiveness is given, but trust is <u>earned</u>. That's why this hurts my feelings. What have I done to deserve such distrust? I have sheltered him, loved him, and never treated him cruelly. But once the other things that were close to him were removed, it has become obvious he doesn't trust <u>me</u>.

This gives us a little glimpse of why God does some of the things He does. He gives…and gives. He's truly the GIVER of life and all good things.

He does it because He LOVES and He desires a relationship with us. But in His infinite wisdom, He sees and knows what we don't. He sees where we've put our trust…in our church…in what we possess… friendships…talents…job…etc. Any one of these things gets removed and we are shaken to the core, and our distrust of God becomes apparent. We blame God for our discomforts and our pain, and we withdraw from Him when all He desires is to draw us to HIMSELF. HE wants to be our confidence instead of us having our confidence and self-worth in something else.

I just got a small taste of how I hurt the heart of God when I run from Him. When I reached for the water hose and Zeke ran off as if I had beaten him with it…it hurt. And when I called and called for him and he hid from me as if I was a monster…that hurt. All I wanted was to clean him up so he could go with me. We run from God and hide…when all He's wanting is to clean us up so we can be with Him. It's a matter of trust. Trust or lack thereof is a fairly accurate gauge of the depth of a relationship. How much do we truly trust God?

MEET EARL

Once I was given a pet squirrel. He was a cutie…you know, a rodent with a fluffy tail. His name was Earl—Earl the squirrel. I took him to the livestock show, and it made me a kid magnet deluxe. I had plenty of "squirrel sitters" among all the cute little 4-H kids running around. Earl was a hit.

Isn't it amazing how a common thing like a squirrel can attract so much "ohh's and ahh's" from people who are used to seeing them outside their windows daily? The reason being that even though we're USED to squirrels, we're NOT used to being able to hold and handle them up close! Suddenly the common squirrel becomes an uncommon experience!

At the risk of sounding degrading, that's an example of what God is doing in the earth right now. Most people in America have at least an inner belief that there is a God. That's common knowledge among most people. God…as a belief…is an everyday, common thing. But God coming CLOSE…being FELT…and even "handled" by His people is something else entirely! God "moving upon and resting upon" His own people is entirely more exciting than just knowing about Him from afar, or believing that a traditional church service is an accurate gauge of what God is like. A squirrel in a tree is one thing…a squirrel on my shoulder is quite another!

God is doing a thing that's going to set many people in "shock mode"…He's coming near. His desire is to be PERSONAL with us! If you'll let Him, He will come close. He will come upon you, rest on you, and ROCK your world!!

Some people meeting Earl were fearful. Some of you are afraid of God like that. You're afraid of Him coming too close. You want God to stay at a "safe" distance…see Him only through stained glass windows. I'm telling you, God is bored of that!! He wants to come CLOSE!! He wants to leave His scent on you! The essence of God on someone is more uncommon than a squirrel on someone's shoulder and will draw far more attention! This world NEEDS God to come close, but He must have a person to come UPON! Are you that person? Are you unsatisfied with gazing at God from a "safe" distance? If so, tell Jesus "I'm here, I'm hungry for You…I want MORE!!" Invite Him to come <u>CLOSE</u>!

Colt Wrangler on a practice bull

**Colt Wrangler's motorcycle shop
in New Braunfels, TX 2017**

TREE OF KNOWLEDGE

We have in our possession at the moment a two-year-old colt.

It's time for him to begin his entrance into "manhood." There's a PURPOSE for this colt, and he'll never fulfill that purpose living according to his own appetites. So, among other things, he's spending time tied to the "tree of knowledge."

Our oldest son, Tyger, who's at West Point, has been experiencing his own "tree of knowledge" time while fulfilling on-post guard duty. On-post guard duty is basically where cadets are scheduled to "guard" something that doesn't need guarding. They just stand there for two hours…guarding nothing…with no bullets…with no enemy to guard against…but they are "guarding." The winters in New York are quite different from those that this Texas boy is used to. Snow on the ground and snow falling, as was the temperature, and his last session was scheduled for 11:00 p.m. to 1:00 a.m. I think Tyger said something like, "Mom, it's STUPID! It serves NO PURPOSE!"

No purpose, huh? If you mean, what are you accomplishing? You're right…nothing. But you've missed the point. It's not about doing or accomplishing ANYTHING! It's about BECOMING. I asked Tyger why we tied colts out. His answer was "OH!" Bingo! Same reason. The colt doesn't learn correct moves or gain knowledge about various equine events…but don't mistakenly think it's of no purpose. The character of the colt is being shaped, altered, and strengthened. Patience is replacing the need to be entertained. Temper tantrums brought on by being inconvenienced are burned away by the sheer immovability of what they're tied to.

I thoroughly enjoyed watching this stud colt get so mad at being tied to a sapling that he stomped and kicked, working up quite a sweat. He pulled at the sapling with his best efforts…only to have the sapling patiently and consistently pull back…Immovable. He had more than met his match. I went about my business while the colt fought with himself. I smiled as I saw the colt eventually give in to his situation. His body language changed from obstinate to yielded. His head lowered, his eyes half shut while resting one back leg. What a difference just simply being made to stand can make!

I can just imagine the leaders at West Point doing the same… looking out their window occasionally to watch a young cadet going through the very same attitudes that a colt tied to a tree goes through. I can almost see a smile cross their lips as they watch impatience and inner frustrations being burned out of youthful cadets, and in its place, an inner yielding to the authority over their lives.

The tree of knowledge in the Bible brought death. The "tree of knowledge" in this context also deals death, but in a GOOD sense. This tree of knowledge implements death to self-importance and selfish attitudes, such as "it's not MY idea and I'm not happy about it!" All the learning in the world does a person no good if their character isn't strong enough to support where their intellect and personal abilities take them.

I find myself from time to time kicking at a situation that I find infuriating. When I've thrown my best fits and the situation still remains, it's time to re-evaluate…maybe God is not out to change my situation so much as He is out to change ME!

Colt Wrangler and
Tyger Tuff
West Point
Graduation

Evening dinner
at West Point

An INCREDIBLE weekend for West Point graduation!

Stud Ponies, Scars, and Finding Destiny

When I was growing up, my dad purchased a Shetland pony that was still a stud. Smart, huh! I had MORE INCIDENTS with that pony! He clotheslined me more than once, kicked me more than once, left me in the dirt more than once…I found myself walking a few miles home… more than once. One time, he actually reared up and struck me in the shoulder, knocking me to the ground, and proceeded to stand over me with his mouth full of MY FLESH until someone ran to my rescue and beat him off me! I loved that pony…though I don't know why…but looking back I definitely think he should have been cut…somewhere around his throat latch. One thing is for sure…if there was a way for horses to have become a bad experience for me, he was it! None of those things helped me learn correct horse handling, but what it DID do for me was take away any fear of facing something rough. It prepared me for a portion of my calling which involved rodeo. Falling off wasn't something to be so afraid of. Later on when I was riding rough stock, bulls and broncs didn't have the same intimidating effect on me that they often had on the other girls. I'd already experienced many "wrecks," and my God had shown Himself faithful to cover me through them all. I had a confidence in God's ability more than my own.

You see, when we submit our lives to the Supremacy of the Lord's hand, we can rest assured that NOTHING is wasted in life's experiences…nothing. Even the bad experiences…things that should never have happened to us…can be of positive use if we'll stop grieving over the event and its effects and start trusting God to make something of us in the midst of it all. You can either let that injury rule your life negatively or you can overcome in Christ so that you can be the instrument that brings healing and hope to other people who've experienced similar things. What buried others can be healed in you so that you are a stronger person, one who fears less and loves more! Is it easy? Nothing of greater value is. But what the devil meant to kill you with can be the VERY EXPERIENCE that makes you UNCONQUERABLE in some field or another!

I can tell story after story of horse mishaps…maybe you can tell heart-wrenching stories of being cruelly abused. My experiences can entertain…YOURS have the power to heal and change lives!! The greater the pain you went through and survived, the greater the value of the GOLD you can impart to other wounded people. Our experiences give us authority when submitted to the Lord. Don't "check out" in life because of a bad experience. Not all people can face life's hard knocks and find who they are in the process, but maybe you are one of those who CAN! Think about it. The very thing that buried other people just might be the pathway to your calling in life!

Rowdy, one of the many pet raccoons I've raised.

Inner Mind-Sets That Sabotage Our Future

Be aware of inner mind-sets. These are the little foxes that spoil the vine—the inner mind-sets or agreements that we have made within ourselves as a result of traumatic events in our lives. "I'll never love again" or "I'll never allow someone to have my heart" or "I'll never be _______________ again." You fill in the blank.

These are covenants, agreements that we made with lower level thinking because of a hurtful experience. Problem is, we CANNOT live above our thinking, and if we think this way, then we have assigned ourselves to live BELOW a certain LOW STANDARD.

Unknowingly we have just assigned ourselves a position within a substandard lifestyle that cannot be changed until these agreements (contracts) are broken, and we consciously come out of agreement with them. As a man thinks within himself, so is he (Proverbs 23:7). Our inner thoughts project outwardly, captivating or repelling like or opposite mind-sets. Allow me to explain. A person who has been rejected (and who hasn't??) and has become convinced within themselves that "no one likes me really," "It's only a matter of time and they'll turn on me like everyone else," etc. THIS thinking is an invisible signal to everyone they come in contact with, and they will find themselves being responded to accordingly. If you think you have no value to people, you won't. If you think you'll be overlooked, you will. If you think you'll always be poor and "everyone else gets the breaks, but never me," you have just sabotaged your pathway to financial freedom. Great opportunities will come your way, but you'll not recognize them; a position presents itself and unbeknownst to you, your poor mentality actually disqualifies you from operating together with a team of money makers, risk takers, entrepreneurs, and inventors. You think you just keep getting a bum rap, but it's actually a covenant that you agreed with long ago that holds you captive to a lower level.

There's a higher way of thinking, but as long as these inner agreements are not dealt with, you and I can't see it. We only think as high as our past experiences. IN DOING SO, WE ALLOW OUR PAST EXPERIENCES TO BE OUR STANDARD. God's ways are not our ways. His thoughts are higher than our thoughts (Isaiah 55:7–9). We can come out of agreement with lower level thinking, and as a result, we can dismiss our own jailer and walk free from a substandard life. Whether it's in finances, or relationships, or a multitude of other areas, the sky is really the limit. But the answer isn't out there…it's actually within myself. Clean house within my own mind-sets and attitudes, and a pathway is cleared for a brighter future! But beware of thinking you can simply "think positively" and it'll be done. While positive thinking is certainly a good habit, it will NOT break you free. You must quiet yourself and spend time (usually more than once), asking God to reveal past experiences that you have allowed to shape your thinking and confine you to a lower standard. If you honestly open yourself up to Him this way and give Him time, He will bring instances of painful memories where you consequently made an agreement of some sort as a result. At that moment, you must break that agreement, forgive, release all involved, and come OUT OF AGREEMENT with that mind-set. It's really as simple as that. Never to go back into agreement with it again.

By doing so, you've just took the lid off your capacity to go higher, live better, healthier, happier.

Colt Wrangler's work has gotten him quite a bit of publicity; several magazine articles plus one program in the TV series, *Ride With Norman Reedus*.

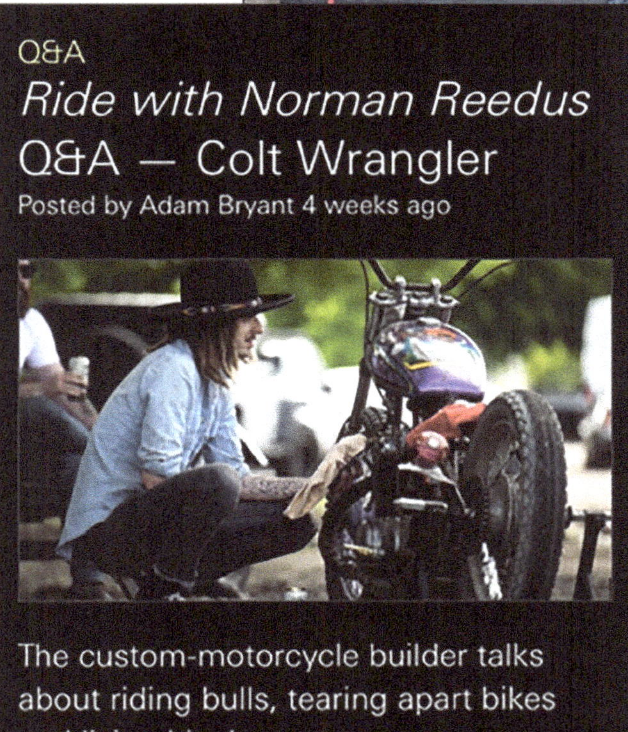

Q&A
Ride with Norman Reedus
Q&A — Colt Wrangler
Posted by Adam Bryant 4 weeks ago

The custom-motorcycle builder talks about riding bulls, tearing apart bikes and living his dream.

Contagious Patriotism

I was at a Memorial Day program being held at the Mason, Texas, courthouse square. Names were read of our local men and women now serving in the military, and a 21-gun salute was given to those who had died serving our country. This was followed by the playing of taps. Throughout the short ceremony, traffic continued as normal, but when taps was played, someone passing through our little town stopped their car in the road. For the duration of taps, traffic stopped. And though it's a major highway going through our town, no one honked or got impatient as all traffic stopped in both directions to honor those fallen and gave respect to those who have given all. It stirred my heart and brought tears welling up in my eyes.

I thought if I were driving through, would I have even been aware that taps was playing in solemn honor to our heroes? Because of the awareness of one person, all were made aware. I wanted to run out and thank whoever that was. I'll lay odds it was a veteran. Those who have paid a price hold in high honor the price that others have paid.

I want to be that one person who stops the flow of traffic and makes others aware that there are more important things than rushing through life unthankful for the sacrifices that paid for our freedom. A sixty-second stop in traffic changed the atmosphere and momentarily put everyone's priorities in check. It was a speed bump in our day, jolting us back to awareness of what's really important. We could use a lot more "speed bumps" like that. People who will take the lead and stand up for what's right. People who are willing to stop the "flow of traffic" to give honor to those deserving of honor, making those who are otherwise oblivious to the fact aware of something they desperately need to be made aware of. These are people who've got their head on straight, who aren't willing to go with the flow when they see that the "flow" is going the wrong way.

When all of society is on a mad rush through life, maybe the most important thing we could become is a "godly speed bump"—a person who causes others to stop and become aware of things more important than a life spent selfishly. The person who stopped traffic that day has no idea that I am writing about him. All those who stopped haven't got a clue how their actions affected me and so many others. It was a natural reaction born of a heart that regards honor. They have probably forgotten all about the incident, but I haven't.

When honor is embraced in someone's heart, others are affected by it. Patriotism is POWERFUL! Wherever the sacrifice of others is held in honor, the effect of patriotism is contagious!

Old Glory is still honored at rodeos and western events!

Superstitions

Superstitions are everywhere, and rodeo is no different. Rough stock riders won't compete in yellow shirts because it's bad luck, and a cowboy NEVER lays his hat on a bed for fear of bucking off. Superstitions. A long time ago, I entered the bull riding event at an all-girl rodeo in Seguin, Texas. I lived in Missouri at the time, so figuring out entry fees and mileage, I came to the distressing realization that I had less than $4 left over to eat on for the whole trip. Sleeping in the car was not a problem with me—but not eating was! I wanted to go bad! (I look back at it now and think, "What in the world made me want to do that?" Proof that youth is wasted on the young!) Anyway, I came up with a plan. I bought a jar of peanuts and marked the jar according to the days I would be gone, so that I would only eat that day's allotment. That way, if I bucked off (which I figured was very likely), I'd have something to eat coming back. I drew a young bull that had antlers—not horns, y'all—antlers! Each horn had to be over three feet long! And to top that off, he was a waspy, hooky, chute-fighting little sucker! Y'all, I'm a long way from home, and I'd like to eat a meal—I can't afford fear! I laid my hands on his hip area (while he's trying to hook me, climb out of the chute, flip over, etc.), and I began claiming Psalm 8:6–7, which says God has given me authority over the beasts of the field. I commanded a spirit of peace to come upon this bull in the Name of Jesus. He instantly quit fighting and settled down. I climbed down on his back, nodded my head, and won the bull riding!! (My get-off was sorry, but at that point, who cares?) When I was gathering up my gear, some young cowboys were talking to me, and I offered them what was left of my jar of peanuts. One of them piped up and said, "Oh, no! Don't you know? Eating peanuts is bad luck!"

I said, "Look, dipstick! I just won the bull riding, and I ate peanuts all the way here!"

With that, they ALL wanted the jar—figuring it was good luck! If I'd been smart, I would've offered them to the highest bidder! The peanuts weren't the point at all! If I would have bucked off, it wouldn't have been because I ate peanuts! It would have been simply because I didn't ride as good as the bull bucked—that's all.

I used to, on purpose, lay my hat down on beds and compete in a yellow shirt—just to prove that superstitions have no validity. The only power they have over us is what we give them! It's a mental distraction that a serious competitor cannot afford. And as a believer in the Lord Jesus Christ, I will not dishonor Him by allowing some superstitious old wives' tale to have any bearing over my mind and emotions. Even if it's all in fun, I can't afford to allow superstitions to have any sway over me because if I do, somewhere down the line, it will steal from me my courage—right when I need it most. I left the arena that evening and headed straight for a steak house!!

You know, to this day, I don't care to eat peanuts.

Photo session for music CD...thanks to Amazing Grace Photography.

MASON, TEXAS, JACKASS RACE

Here in Mason, we have an annual jackass race. Yep, it's our town's claim to fame. Not really. The next town just north of us, Brady, has an annual "World Championship Goat Cook-Off." I'm not really sure where they get the "world" part, but it does possibly cover surrounding states, and although the contest is dominated by Texans, nobody is safe in ANY cooking contest when Cajuns from Louisiana show up!

How'd I get off on food?? Oh well, back to Mason's annual jackass race. It's quite the event! They line the donkeys up (sort of), and the race begins with a shotgun blast. I think that's for the purpose of encouraging the little beasts to possibly start faster. The race is one full lap around the courthouse square. Have you ever SEEN a jackass race? It's not an adrenaline rush by any stretch. Most of the time, just to get one donkey to complete the race, two or three people are involved simply to keep the little guy motivated and going the right direction! I can promise you this, the people involved for the duration of the race have worked FAR harder than the donkeys! You could finish the race much faster if you just got off and went on foot! But that's not the point. It's just a Texas thang, y'all! The courthouse square is jammed with people, and at every side street there's mounted cowboys…outriders stationed with ropes in hand just in case a donkey goes AWOL. Off they go as the crowd gets involved in the events happening along the journey and caring nothing about who actually wins the race. That's the fun of this race—if you can even call this a race—to simply enjoy the inevitable funny stunts along the way.

It's more like watching a herd of stampeding turtles.

What if we could have the same motivation in life? Where we pay far more attention just to the journey itself instead of being so preoccupied with who gets first prize? And about donkeys themselves, why do we regard them as being below our "worthy gaze?" Fact is, the humble I remember reading about a donkey that could see and know the purposes of God and spoke with wisdom! The very gifted prophet riding her was blinded to the very real danger he was in because of his own greed for profit and position. What about the donkey carrying Jesus into Jerusalem? Wow…if I could attain to that level of usefulness…to be a faithful carrier of the King of Glory. Remember how all the people were laying their garments on the ground for the donkey to walk on and waving palm branches along the procession in praise? What an ass that donkey would have been if he had the audacity to think all was for him! How many of us could pass THAT test? That donkey cared nothing for all the fanfare; he was simply the carrier of the KING. My…to be more like a donkey!

What's my ass-piration?? (I couldn't resist.) Simply to be more like the two donkeys mentioned above. I'd like to have my spiritual eyes opened to see and know what God is doing, so as to not be moving contrary to His purposes. I'd like to have the wisdom of a donkey to realize it's the Presence of the King I carry that's the most valuable asset in my life! Come to think of it…to be like a DONKEY ain't such a bad deal!

BULL IN THE CHICKEN HOUSE

Where's the camera when you need one? I heard the chickens going ape-snerd and ran out to see what was the matter. The longhorn bull was inside the chicken house, calmly eating hay out of the nests and licking up the laying pellets out of the hanging feeder while the chickens were bouncing off the walls. It was a Kodak moment. While crazed chickens where flying over his back, the bull quietly turned his head sideways so he could fit his horns through the door and come back out. I am sure that egg production will be down for a day or so.

How did it happen? Well, a small gate was left open—that is all it took to give me a laugh, and the chickens something to cackle about for a few hours. Did you know that not every open door is to be walked through? I've heard people say, "I knew it must be God because it just opened up for me!" Heck, I've said those words myself! Some of those "open doors" that I walked through, thinking they were "God," left a memory that isn't near as funny to me as the bull in the chicken house—although come to think of it, it did give folks something to cackle about for a while.

God wants us to be led by His Spirit, that still, quiet-sounding voice down on the inside of us that we can brush off as "nothing" if we don't watch it, NOT some "open door." Some open doors **are** God! But the point is, we are not to be led by them. I have walked through some of those open doors before and been just as out of my element and in the wrong place as that bull was in the chicken house. Problem was, it took me a lot longer to get back out! Although I gotta say, I *have* learned some valuable lessons because of it. One of which is: Even though a bull eats all the laying pellets, he still won't lay eggs.

Peacocks...and Other Wrecks

I have always LOVED peacocks. I love driving up at someone's ranch headquarters with huge trees around their house and barn, seeing (and hearing) peacocks in the trees announcing your arrival. But no matter how beautiful a thing is…in its wrong place or time…it can be a painful thing. My painful peacock story happened during a season when I was breezing horses on someone's personal track. They owned a barn full of young racehorses that I was hired to exercise daily. They also owned several dogs, cats, chickens, turkeys, and peacocks that freely roamed the place. I loved all the critters and the atmosphere they each add to an environment.

As you may already know, young race colts aren't usually the most well-broke animals. It was a daily thing to ride through the knots in their back, and the usual "pitching" that had to be worked out before actually expecting a good breeze around the track. One of the fillies was especially flighty, and she was also BIG, but other than darting one way or the other as she dodged her imagined boogers, she was no trouble, and she could stretch out and run! One such day I was enjoying her stride as we were at a full gallop and rounding the corner at one end of the track. All I actually remember was seeing a peacock streak across the track in front of us and the filly's head disappearing. She went from a stretched-out run to swallowing her head and trying to elevate herself to rooftop level while hitting reverse. I just remember seeing her ears from an airborne position prior to kissing the ground face-first. I don't know how long I was knocked out because no one was there to see what happened. But when I DID come to, I found the filly peacefully grazing in the center area of the track. Whether I was out minutes or hours, I have no idea, but my bell had been rung royally because after catching the mare and leading her back to the barn, I discovered that I had NO MEMORY of which horses I had already ridden and which horses I hadn't. No horses were even best to just let it go…no more riding that day.

Have you ever made note of how sometimes something "beautiful" that you've always wanted in life can show up at the wrong time? Or in the wrong package? A person shows up in your life that's EXACTLY what your heart has been searching for all your life…but they're married. Or the job you've dreamed of having appears, but you have to be LESS than honorable to shift from the job you're at to get this one. Just like a peacock…it doesn't matter how BEAUTIFUL it is…if it shows up at the wrong place or time and you engage it, it will very well end in a massive WRECK. ANYTHING YOU COMPROMISE TO GET, YOU MUST CONTINUE COMPROMISING TO KEEP. Or Biblically speaking, "Everything produces after its own kind." No matter how "beautiful" something is, if you attain it "illegally" (by that, I mean being less than honorable), it will eventually come back around to bite you in the butt. No matter how beautiful it is, if it's coming to you "sideways" (like that peacock), it's a TRAP…DON'T BITE! You may "fly high" for a time, but you'll eventually come down. And I don't need to tell you how painful it can be when the reality of ground level hits home.

His to Win...Mine to Wear

I have won a few buckles, but none that I like to wear as much as the ones my son has won. They are newer, prettier, and well...simply COOLER! As I was putting on a belt with Colt Wrangler's buckle attached to it, I got to thinking about this whole scenario.

Colt had to discipline himself to practice and put out the effort to drive the long distances to rodeos. He had to face the challenges of getting on both bulls and broncs. He had to deal with facing his fears and overcoming mental blockages. He had to carry the injuries that riding rough stock always incurs, and that kid worked a job from fourteen years old and up to pay his own entry fees, as much as was possible for him to do. And I am wearing the trophies of his hard work and efforts!

My favorite saddle is the one Colt Wrangler won his senior year in saddle broncs. That's the saddle I ride in all the events I do. I didn't get on one bronc, but I sure am enjoying the saddle that he won in that event! We gathered up horses that were renegades...anything that we could find...for him to practice on. We bucked out in arenas that hadn't had the ground worked in MONTHS...hard as concrete...and that kid hit the dirt over and over again, never giving up. I now sit my butt in a saddle that didn't cost me one bruise! He paid the price for what I enjoy!

I didn't have to crawl down on one bull...not one...and yet I wear the buckles from that event that he won! Colt Wrangler spent $1,200 of his own hard-earned money to buy one terrific little practice bull that would go both ways. "Mighty Mo" was an AWESOME practice bull, easy to handle and very rideable as long as you didn't make any mistakes. If you rode correctly, you could get by him easily enough...but get sloppy and you were out of there. Also, Mo worked really hard to not step on a kid even when they were right under him. Mo was perfect for the job! Because of that, Colt's investment was a blessing to several other boys who kept trying their luck on good 'ole Mo.

I never once had to get on the bull, though I did flank him a bunch. I never spent the time in the hospital that Colt had to recuperating from broken bones dealt him by a bull. But I wear the buckles….

This is exactly like what is offered to every person by Jesus! HE was tortured and spit on and rejected by those He loved…He went to hell and defeated Satan on his own turf. HE walked in a world FULL of hate and injustices and temptations and never faltered…NOT ONCE! HE won the prize that I am now invited to WEAR! I have access as a child of God to ALL that Jesus WON! It's not mine to win…it's mine to wear! Jesus WON it so I could WEAR it!! It was HIS to win…it's mine to WEAR!

I LOVE wearing the anointing and power that He paid the price for!! I lavish in the supreme HONOR of wearing His nature…possessing His heart…hearing His voice…and experiencing His PEACE! It was HIS to win…but it's MINE TO WEAR!!! Sooooo…dress yourself in what Jesus has won for you! You can't EARN it…but you were meant to WEAR it!

Tyger and I celebrating Colt winning TX Region 6 Saddle Bronc title for 2010

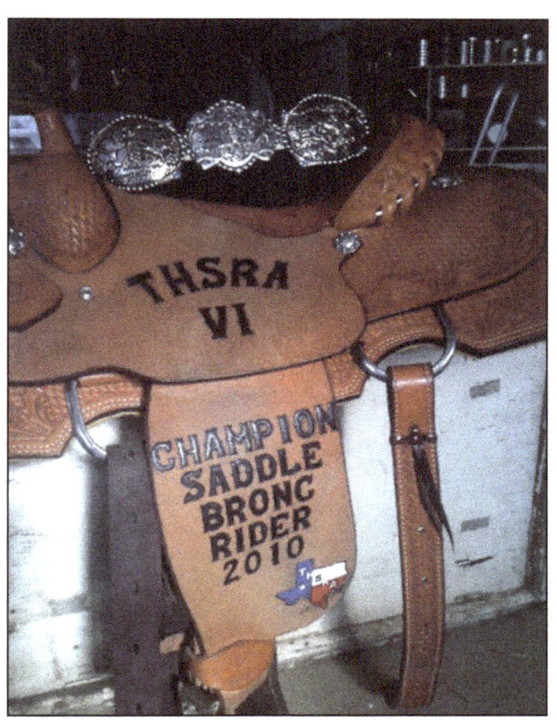

Colt Wrangler
at Texas High
School Rodeo
Finals, Abilene,
TX 2010

Colt Wrangler at Region 6 Texas High School Rodeo 2010

Texas High School Rodeo Finals, Abilene, TX 2010

FACING FEAR

Everyone, without exception, faces fear. How we handle it is the million-dollar question! I learned something years ago, when I was rodeoing, that has continued to be a great blessing in my life. I was entered in the goat tying at a rodeo in Mountain View, Arkansas, and I suddenly became plagued with thoughts of wrecking. I had gone through a pretty serious knee injury before because of tying goats, and I could see myself coming off the horse, falling, tearing up another knee, and just overall making a complete fool of myself. It was not a pretty mental picture. I kept fighting it, but fear began to grip me like claws. I literally felt like a dark wet blanket of fear was over me, and it was suffocating. I began to think, "This is a warning from God," so I was contemplating turning out. I went off on the rodeo grounds to pray, and God began to talk to me. You know, not an audible voice, but that still, peaceful whisper you hear down inside. He began to tell me that the fear I was feeling was not mine. Well, I sure felt I could argue with Him there! It FELT like mine! He went on to teach me that fear is a spirit—a demon spirit—and when it comes into our presence, we feel "it." The fear we feel is the "presence of fear itself"—a spirit of fear. He began to encourage me to not let it enter in (it felt like it already had!) and to face the very thing that it was telling me NOT to do. Do the thing you fear, and fear must leave! (Understand, I am afraid of snakes—this doesn't mean I'm supposed to go find one and play with it!) There's good fear, like not standing in the street—and bad fear. Know the difference.

Anyway, I began quoting 2 Timothy 1:7—"God has not given me a spirit of fear, but of power, love, and a sound mind." I said it over and over, right up to the time for me to ride into the arena and tie my goat. (This was over an hour at least.) I STILL felt afraid. But as soon as I rode my horse into the arena and headed for the goat, all fear left! I won the goat tying that day!

Years later, I was riding bulls in the Women's Pro Rodeo Association and was entered at Bell Fourche, South Dakota. It was a PRCA rodeo that had us girls competing also, and two guys had already been carted off to ICU. The girl just ahead of me in bulls was a Canadian. Her bull fell with her, busted her up all over, and she was the third person to go to ICU! I'm next to go out on my bull. Fear is so thick you could cut it with a knife! (Right about this time is when I wished I had liked playing with dolls instead of liking the tomboy stuff!) I kept quoting a verse out of Psalm 91—"A thousand shall fall at my side and ten thousand at my right hand, but it shall NOT COME NEAR ME!" I still FELT afraid! It wasn't until I nodded my head and called for the gate, that the gripping feeling of fear left me. I was the only girl that whole weekend to cover a bull, so I won the whole pot!

Learn to discern fear's presence. When you know it's the wrong kind of fear, speak the Word, ask for God's help, and DO what fear is telling you NOT to do!! There's a blessing in it!

I won the rodeo on this bull at Belle Fourche, SD in 1987 after fighting off fear by quoting a verse from Psalm 91.

Sowing the Good While You Reap the Bad

Ever walked through a time in your life when you suddenly "woke up" and became aware of your uncomfortable circumstances?

And to make matters worse, the pain of the realization that things were like this because of choices <u>you</u> had made and seeds <u>you</u> had sown? If you have, join the ranks! It's at this point in time that we have a chance to CHANGE our choices, "sow different seed." It's painfully obvious to someone with the IQ equal to room temperature that if you don't like the crop you have been reaping, CHANGE WHAT YOU ARE SOWING! It's at this place in many people's lives that they do just that; where they have been living in rebellion, or laziness, selfishness, etc., they repent and turn around. Where their life was going in one direction, they are now going in the opposite direction. Problem is—what we continue to reap does not cease to exist at the exact moment we change what we're sowing! This is a time of transition that's TOUGH! There will be quite a little time where you continue to have to handle tough situations, hard times, bad repercussions from past sins and mistakes WHILE you are doing the <u>right</u> thing! This is where most people fail the test. They think, "Hey, I'm doing the right thing and where is it getting me?" What they don't realize is that just because we START sowing right seeds, it doesn't mean we get an instant "crop failure" of all the bad seeds we've sown! This time in our lives takes diligence. We've got to take on the attitude that we are going to do the right thing whether it benefits us or not, just because it's RIGHT! That attitude of heart and mind will set the course for great blessings on down the road. Only the faithful will reap those blessings. We live in such an "instant" society that's fueled by the attitude of "what's in it for me?" where if we don't get instant rewards and gratification, we lose heart and go back to our ways that got us into this mess in the first place! Why is it so hard? It's designed by God to be this way! As a result, our motives are tested and purified. Only those who desire change for the right reasons will make it!

For those of you who see yourself in this scenario, take courage! The tough times won't linger forever! The issue isn't just getting the monkey off your back. The issue is becoming who God wants you to be and living a life that fulfills your God-given destiny! For those of you who would rather die headed in the direction of freedom than live another day as a slave to sin and its repercussions, God has given a word—"And let us not be weary in well doing; for in <u>due season</u>, we shall reap, IF WE FAINT NOT" (Gal. 6:9).

STAY STEADY ON COURSE!

**Dancing with Tyger at the Cowboy
Christmas Ball, Anson, TX 2014**

HAVE YOU SWALLOWED A WOODEN EGG?

The other day I was out at the henhouse collecting eggs and found myself face-to-face with a big black chicken snake all coiled up in a nest. That'll get your heart rate going! Well, we killed him. (I watched from a safe distance.) He had a big lump in him where he had swallowed one of the wooden eggs I keep in the nests. Talk about a severe case of constipation! He thought he was getting something that was going to fill his hunger, but instead he got something that would slowly kill him. He didn't know it, but what he had taken in was a death sentence. That egg had the smell of chicken on it, but it was a decoy.

Have you swallowed something that is killing you? Are you mad at someone? Have you taken on an attitude of resentment and bitterness against someone? Boy, don't it feel good when you just let your emotions go and fly off the handle at someone who—of course—deserves it! Yeah, buddy, it feels real good! It feels good going down, but it's kinda like that wooden egg—if you don't get it out of you, it'll kill you! The longer it's allowed to stay, the greater harm it does, and the greater we're in danger of passing a point of no return.

I've heard it said that a man who holds on to resentment and won't forgive is like a man drinking poison and hoping the guy he's mad at gets sick! You gotta get it out of you. Forgiveness is NOT a feeling! It's a decision. You give the incident AND the offender over to God and you let it go, releasing them of the debt of offence that they owe you. It's hard, yeah. About like coughing up that wooden egg! But it's better than dying as a result of it. Oh, you may not lose your life physically, but you'll lose joy, vision, peace, hope. You'll forfeit the hand of God on your life. That's right, you hold on to grudges and unforgiveness, and God has to remove Himself from your presence. Jesus even went so far as to say in Matthew 6:14–15, that if you would not forgive those who've sinned against you, God in heaven could not forgive you of your sins! That means, that at the end of my life, there is NO HOPE of heaven, only hell. It ain't worth it! Forgiving people means coughing up my pride—my right to be avenged! Coughing up pride is as hard as regurgitating that wooden egg! Hey, whatever it takes to get that source of death out of my system is worth it!

**Getting to celebrate West Point's 100th Night with my son.
What a privilege!**

MY TIMES ARE IN YOUR HANDS

I have found that as we interact with our kids, animals, other people, and situations, etc., God will often use what we're dealing with as a picture sermon. This has rung true many times in my life. Years ago, I was delivering a kitten to its new home, and as kittens sometimes do in a vehicle, this little guy was getting disturbed and wanted OUT. He began pressing his nose up against the window, and you could easily see the source of his frustration. He could SEE where he wanted to be, but an invisible barrier was between where he was and where he wanted to go. His frustration mounted, and I began to talk to him as if he understood every word. I started telling him how that I was taking him someplace he was gonna love, but if he was to get out BEFORE I got him there, it would be disastrous for him. Just then, the Spirit of God nudged me inwardly as if to say, "That's EXACTLY what I'm doing with you!" Then I distinctly heard Him say that I should enjoy this time of SLOWNESS because a time was coming when life would move so speedily I would be asking Him to slow things down. Everything I heard that day from the Spirit of God through that kitten incident proved to be exactly right on. Years later, I was reminded of it when I found myself asking God to "slow things down a bit!"

Two days ago, as I was walking across a gravel parking lot in the hot Oklahoma sun, I came upon a baby bird. He was panting horribly in the heat. Well, shoot, I just couldn't LEAVE him there! So I carried the little guy to my trailer and got an eye dropper to get some water in him and filled his little belly with some canned dog food I had. After only having him a couple of days, it was easy to see WHY he was where he was! That little guy wants to fly SO BAD! He KNOWS he's supposed to be able to fly, so off he jumps…and down he goes. He's starting to get feathers, but he doesn't yet have what it's going to take to keep him airborne. He's frustrated because he can FEEL that this nest is NOT where he's supposed to live his life, but he's not yet capable of handling the world he so desperately wants to plunge into! I've named him Rowdy. I have no idea if he even IS a he, but Rowdy is his/her name nonetheless.

I can't EVEN begin to tell you how that little bird so expresses where I'm at right now! After a couple days of taking care of him, I began to get it. I KNOW that I'm destined for more than where I am right now. Maybe you can relate to this also. This little guy getting out of his nest before he's capable of flying is a recipe for disaster, and the same goes for you and me. The frustrating part of destiny is KNOWING you were meant to "fly" long before you develop the necessary equipment it takes to carry you! It's easy to get ahead of God. We get impatient…but if we step out too early, we make ourselves vulnerable to the enemy, and we may NEVER experience what God intended. Have you noticed how the Word of God constantly tells us to WAIT on the Lord? Hmmm…maybe there's something to that!!

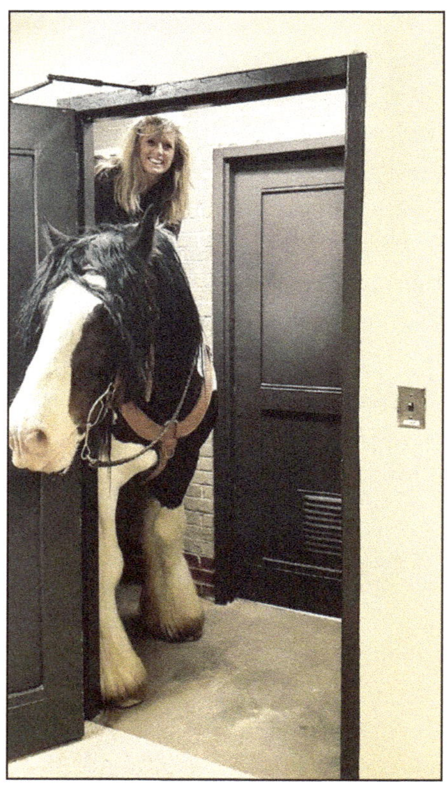

Just checking in with the secretary at an event.

A couple of hang-ups, Billings, MT 1986
Not a fun day at the office!

Who's Yo' Daddy?

There's a story in Genesis about a young boy, Isaac, who was very deeply wounded by the hatred and rejection of his older half-brother, who wanted Isaac's inheritance. Many years later, when Isaac's own sons were being born (twins), the younger came out with his hand grasping his older brother's ankle. That innocent action immediately stirred up old hurts, angers, and fears in Isaac, and he named his younger son Jacob. It means "trickster, supplanter, cheater." From the day of Jacob's birth, he felt the curse of his father. Why? Because what we don't get over and get healed of, we pass on to our kids. Jacob SHOULD have received acceptance, love, and encouragement from his father, but instead, nothing Jacob did ever gained his father's approval.

What complicates the situation further is that God has ordained that the father be the one who blesses his children. He has been empowered by God to speak strength, encouragement, and blessing into the lives of his children. It's bad enough when this isn't done, but when it is reversed and the father only curses his children, the effects can be devastating for generations to come!

This story has a good ending, however, and yours can too. In Genesis 32, Jacob has an experience with God that changes all this and his life forever. In this encounter with God, Jacob comes face-to-face with the source of his hurt, and God washes it all away and gives Jacob a new name—Israel, meaning a prince with God and with man. This encounter changes him forever, and you see him passing this blessing on to his children and grandchildren, a blessing in the latter years of his life that to this day is being lived out.

What about you? Are you a father that is blessing your children with your words and actions or cursing them? Did you have a father that blessed you or one who never approved of you? If your "fathering experience" is less than savory, switch your daddy! How can we learn to be good parents when we've been raised by bad ones? God desires to be your Daddy! Learn from Him! Your father didn't show you love? God will. Your father never blessed you with kind words? God will. Your father never saw the worth in you? God does. You have a bad heritage that has left you with undesirable qualities as your inheritance? Psalm 47:4 says God shall choose the inheritance for us that He did for Jacob. Wow! Seek after God! Call upon the name of Jesus and simply ask God to become REAL in your life. Once you have a genuine experience with God, your life will radically change for the better. Don't think that you have to take whatever comes down the line of your natural heritage. You HAVE a choice! You CAN be healed of past wounds, becoming soft where you've been hard, and passing down a blessing to your children instead of passing down your own injuries. Are you living under the influence of your natural father or your Heavenly Father? That will tell it all.

Who's Yo' Daddy?

WHAT KIND OF CAT ARE YOU?

Several years ago, we sold the place where we were living, and you know the scenario—TONS of things to move, cattle to sell, boxes, boxes, and more boxes. The last night we were there, all was done, and we were ready to leave for an extended road trip the next morning. I was pooped! Early that morning, about daylight, the Lord woke me up and moved on me to get out of bed and go outside because He wanted to talk to me. I didn't <u>want</u> to get out of bed! But I got a cup of coffee and headed for the barn. Sitting still and just quietly praying, the cats began to gather around me—and God began to talk.

All these cats liked being <u>around</u> a person, but none would allow you to catch it and hold it—all except for one. That cat hopped up in my lap, let me touch it, pet it, and carry it around. I had already found a home for her to go to, a place where she would be taken care of and safe from what was coming. You see, the folks who bought the ranch had some sure enough salty stock dogs who would make quick work of any cat they could catch. I had spent the last week trying to catch cats so we could move them to a place of safety, but I was unable to catch any. They would let me get <u>close</u>—but don't touch! You see, they liked being **around** me, but they didn't want me **too close**! They didn't desire my touch—they liked the cat feeder staying full—but they wanted to keep their independence. Little did they know that those days of "safe independence" were over. Something was coming on the scene that would unleash destruction in their lives.

I **could** have spared them from what was coming, but they didn't allow it. Was I mad at them? No. Did they **do** anything to deserve what was coming? No. Why did one cat get spared and the others did not? Simply this—ALL the cats liked what I could give. ALL liked having me around. But only ONE would come CLOSE. Only one desired my touch. That one I was able to spare from what was to come—the others, I was not. Did I want to see it happen? Not at all, but it wasn't my choice—it was theirs.

God began speaking to me about the things coming upon the world. Tough and dangerous times are ahead. America will not be exempt. God has many people in America that claim Him as Lord. He has many who call upon the name of Jesus, enjoy the blessings He gives, and like Him being <u>around</u> in their lives—but there are FEW who indeed actually desire to come CLOSE to Him! Few want His touch in their lives. Few want to be submitted to His will and desire. We like His blessings, but we want to retain our independence.

Those who want to be as close as they can possibly be to Him, those who want His touch, will be kept secure, in a safe place. Those who only want what He gives—while keeping a certain amount of independence, will be in a dangerous place. Because God is mad at them? No. Because God loves them less? No. God did not choose their outcome. They did! Did they not "perform" well enough? No. It has nothing to do with "performance." It is based SOLELY on the desire, or lack of desire, to just COME CLOSE.

Do you like the blessings of God in your life, but don't desire to submit to His CONTROL? Or do you hunger for MORE of God—wanting His touch in your life to come in greater degrees? The answer to these questions will let you know where you stand.

What kind of cat are you?

Grabbing the Bit

A long time ago, back in my dumber days—actually, it was when I was a kid—I had this horse that had come off the race track. It was obvious that he had been mistreated and soured. He was a powerful horse, and I loved him. He would do just fine until he got into a situation where he came under pressure, and he would lose it! You never knew when it was gonna happen either. One time at a horse show, he reared up and came down on the hood of someone's little sports car. (Why do parents let their kids ride horses like this?) Anyway we had a few mishaps together but nothing like the one we had in the lot of a Walmart at Sedalia, Missouri.

I had made it to state with this horse, and some friends and I decided to ride from the fairgrounds to Walmart. We got our stuff and were leaving. I had a bag of ice in front of me in the saddle and a spatula in my hip pocket. "Bullwinkle" (he had a head that sorta favored a moose) started getting nervous. I began doing what I always did to calm him, but it wasn't working. Next thing I knew, he had grabbed the bit shank in his mouth and started running 9-0 across the paved parking lot. I knocked the ice out of the saddle and started thinking about my options. We could go right and cross a busy street or hold straight and aim for a big seven-foot chain link fence. I chose the fence, figuring that he would stop. He didn't. He tried to jump it! We landed on the other side upside-down, a couple of sections of fence laid out, and the horse was thrashing around trying to get back on his feet. Some guys across the street at a gas station saw the whole thing, and I could hear them screaming as they were running to us, "She's broke her neck!"

I thought, "Oh my God, I've broke my neck!" But when the dust settled, all I had was a lot of sore places, a busted nose, two black eyes—and a calmer horse.

This horse wasn't born this way. Being handled roughly and mistreated by man had made him like he was. Eventually he came out of it totally and made quite the good ranch horse, but it took time, love, and patience. I've met people like this. Past experiences have wounded them deeply, and when under certain kinds of stress, they flip out, grab the bit, and do things they later regret. There IS a better way.

Yes, we know you've been mistreated and abused, but you can't use this as your ticket in life forever! There has to come a time where we leave our past behind or we can never enjoy our todays, much less have any hope for a better tomorrow! The fact is, if you have TRULY given your life over to Jesus Christ, you now have a new owner—One Who will never abuse you. So if you say you trust Jesus, why not really trust Him? When you find yourself under the gun (so to speak), don't take the bit and go off doing things your own way. Learn to listen and wait on God. He KNOWS what to do—we just "think" we do! Take time to know—really know—your new Master. When you know Him, you can trust Him. Oh, and by the way—spit that bit out!

Tyger didn't want any pictures taken of him shooting a pink AR… but Moms often get their way. He built this gun for me and dragged his feet when I requested it to be PINK.

Every girl
NEEDS
her color-
coordinated
accessories!!

When Tyger was fifteen and lying awake contemplating his love of guns, he wrote this:

TOP 14 REASONS GUNS ARE BETTER THAN GIRLS

1. You can have more than one.

2. You can get one in the color you want, and they won't keep changing.

3. They only rattle off when you want them to.

4. If you get rid of one, you get money back.

5. Accessories are intended for long-term use.

6. Their shape doesn't change with time.

7. They travel much lighter.

8. They can be changed to fit their owner's preference.

9. You can change between high and low velocity ammo at will.

10. A good one is easy to handle.

11. Popular ones are available to everyone.

12. Most can be completely understood in a matter of days.

13. If they lose a screw, it can be replaced.

14. Even the heavy ones look good.

The expression Tyger has when looking at guns
is amazingly similar to you know who!

Tyger with the SCAR 17 he built…he says
"girls love scars!" Whatever!

HAA!

I feel the need to address a very serious issue in the horse industry. Addictions. Most people with addictions aren't even willing to admit they have a problem. That is also the case here. I have found this addiction everywhere in the horse industry at an alarming rate. I have also found it freely covers every area of "horsedom." No discipline is free of its overwhelming effects on our psychological system. The internet has done more to heighten the effects of this malady than anything else in our generation. What kind of addicts am I talking about? Horse addicts. You see them everywhere—they look like everyday, normal, "got it all together" type people—but under the surface they are fighting to find some "anchor in the storm," some sanity, some way to bring about a means to stop drooling over and buying another horse that they don't need. We've tried the "just say no" slogan. It doesn't work.

Did I say "we?" That was a pure slip of the tongue. I personally don't have a problem in this area. I can quit anytime I want to—I just haven't wanted to. But for all you horse addicts out there, I am thinking about starting up an organization called HAA (Horse Addicts Anonymous)! We could form local chapters, get together, and share openly our addiction problem with others who understand. Who knows, if all else fails and we don't find a cure, we can share information with one another on any new avenues that have opened up for the buying and selling of horses! I see this as a "no lose" situation! Plus, as an added incentive, we could have yearly membership dues. That way those of us on the "ground floor" would have a little "extra" in our bank accounts to spend on horses! Hey! We might as well enjoy ourselves while searching for a cure!

How do you know if you've got "it?" Do you find yourself from time to time uncontrollably looking up horse sites on the internet? (My son calls it "internet horse porn.") Do you ever catch yourself saying things like, "Just one more—and then I'll quit"? Do you find yourself looking at another horse when you're not getting the ones you have ridden enough as it is? Is your attitude about owning horses very similar to buying shoes—you need one for every season, one for every special occasion, and one in every color? Do you sometimes wonder how you are going to afford the feed bills, vet bills, training bills…as well as just the normal living expenses, while at the same time you're trying to figure out HOW to get your hands on this other horse you've seen? If you have answered any of these questions with a "yes," YOU have a problem!

Okay, I'm serious about this. We've already discovered that "just saying no" doesn't work. Neither does going around chanting, "I don't need another horse, I don't need another horse!" Soooo why not start up Horse Addicts Anonymous, get our "HAA" sticker, and every time someone is close to selling us another horse, just begin to shout out "H-A-A!" Loudly now! H-A-A! With passion! H-A-A!!!!!!

I'm sure it won't keep us from trying to buy another horse, BUT it just MIGHT keep someone from selling us another horse simply because they will be convinced we're a total nut case! What do ya think? I am open to suggestions.

**Colt Wrangler and I spending a glorious
afternoon on the Sabinal River in Utopia, TX**

Don't Ya Just Love Sheep?...Not!

My sons were in 4-H. Therefore, we were picking out sheep to bring home, feed, halter break, exercise and do the overall "sheep" thing. We got 'em unloaded and in their pen...all except for one. It got loose and began frantically running around looking for its "buds." We got around it and began aiming it in the right direction. It's like sheep take on this attitude—"if you want me to go THIS way...then that MUST be the way I _don't_ want to go!" Its head is up high, its eyes are wide open, but can it see the other sheep right in front of it? Noooo! I have a personal belief that sheep are blind in part. You know, mentally blind. They can see escape routes...things to eat and such, but can't seem to see what NEEDS to be seen! So, she headed out to pasture, bleating all the way. We ran to get around her. She ran farther away. We ran some more...You know the story.

She went under the board fence and got out in the pasture with the horses. Oh GREAT! How do you explain to the breeders that the expensive sheep you borrowed from them is now dead? You don't explain...you just pull out your checkbook. The horses caught sight of the ewe. It was like a herd of cats going after a mouse. Five horses honed in on one sheep, each one intent on relieving it of its misery. The ewe was darting and diving. The horses were all over it. We were running around, arms waving, shouting at one another, huffing and puffing. Welcome to the Lyons' home...where peace and serenity reigns!

Finally the ewe just couldn't go anymore. Tyger was closest and grabbed the sheep...foiling the horses' plans to kill her. We each took turns carrying her out of the death trap she'd gotten herself into and back to the place she belonged. All ended well. The sheep got exercised...WE got exercised...the horses were entertained...so were the neighbors, I'm sure.

The more I hang around sheep, the more I feel insulted that that's what God likened His people to. Why not horses...or eagles...or deer—

something with brains and class! Why sheep? I think I know (though I don't care for the answer). We can be blind in part too...mentally blind. Blind to see only what we WANT to see. The moment we feel God's prodding to move us in a certain direction, we IMMEDIATELY take on the attitude that if God wants me to go THAT way, then I'm sure I won't LIKE it! So we run around in our circles of despair, barely escaping flying hooves coming our way and thinking we've really "cut a shine," until we just can't go any further. Then if we don't get killed in the process, we finally poop out and welcome the Savior...the Rescuer of our souls... the great Shepherd to step in and deliver us. He'll pick us up from where we are and carry us to where we should be...and would have been ALREADY if we hadn't been so bullheaded.

Oh, the life of sheep. Though you and I would like to think of ourselves as "other than," I think our wool is definitely showing.

Have I expressed how much I love my stallion?

POTTY TRAINING = PARENT TRAINING

Both our sons were little when we were on the road full time going from rodeo to rodeo. Our youngest, Colt Wrangler, was born on the road. I was very thankful to have boys during this time. There are definite conveniences in the male gender when living a lifestyle lacking in bathroom availability. They learned at an early age to pee in a juice, Gatorade, or "whatever was available" jar when going down the road.

I remember when we were potty training them, how we had to start with just getting them to pee <u>outside</u> their jeans. We worked on <u>where</u> they peed later…first things first. One such time, one of our sons (I'm withholding names to protect the guilty) was with me while I was going to a nice big grocery store. He began to say he had to go. I'm telling him "hold on," as I'm grabbing things out of the car. I look up just in time to see him peeing on one of the columns of this huge grocery store. People are coming in and out of the store staring at this little guy donned in cowboy hat, boots and spurs, getting some relief. I actually walked a wide circle away from him in hopes no one would know I was his mother! Terrible…I know. He gets done and instantly looks up for the praise that is his reward for a job well done. (i.e., "You did <u>sooo</u> good!" "That was great!" "Wow, what a <u>big</u> boy you are!") He is grinning from ear to ear, so proud of himself that he didn't pee in his jeans. What could I do? I praised him, of course…using some of the above phrases. While it looked to others like he was a naughty boy, he actually had crossed a milestone in trying so hard to do the right thing. I could have killed it at that moment by responding according to "appearances" because of my frustration and <u>pride</u> instead of what was right.

You know, we are all so guilty of wanting a life free of its messes. We can easily get caught up in the facades that society deems so important. Fact is, at that moment, my little boy needed affirmation more than I needed to "look good" in the eyes of others. Our pride and screwed-up value systems can cause so much damage to our little ones! We get so busy in our fast-paced lifestyles that we can completely miss out on some of the most precious moments that endear us to our kids. Sometimes we need to look beyond what they <u>did</u> to see the intentions of their heart. When they are being rebellious…you know it…deal with it. When they are trying their little heart out and yet make a mess of things…they need encouragement, not criticism. God gives that to us and expects us to give it to others along the way…then He gives us kids so we can <u>practice</u> and hopefully start getting it right!

**Tyger and Colt with their "guardian,"
the frosty heeler Nicodemus.**

Snipe Hunting

Oh, the things young people miss out on these days! Remember snipe hunting? Oh yeah…it's a great thing! I remember being at a bunking party once when I was in high school, and we discovered that one of the girls had never gone snipe hunting. We commenced telling her how much fun it was, and presently she was excited about going. We got the "official gear" for the hunt…one unsuspecting person and a tow sack. Out into the woods we headed until we found a suitable place for our dastardly deed. We gave instructions to the victim on how to hold the tow sack open and close to the ground, and how to give out intermittent calls of "here snipe, here snipe" while the rest of us would circle around and herd the snipes in her direction. Off we went and left her, with tow sack in hand, as we giggled all the way back to the house for some hot chocolate. I don't recall just how long we left her out there (I actually think she got lost for a while). What I do remember is how she didn't speak to us for quite some time (some folks just can't take a joke).

Colt reminded me the other day of how I took him snipe hunting… HIS OWN MOTHER!…as he put it. I set him next to the fence line with a feed sack, calling out to the snipes and went back to the house. He stayed there a good while…then came on in. Even a little kid can eventually figure out he's been had. Hey, call me cruel, but I bet I got something done at the house while he was being occupied with thoughts of catching the ever-elusive snipe! We have laughed and laughed over "snipe hunting."

The next summer while working show cattle with other 4-H kids, our boys discovered some kids that had NEVER heard of snipe hunting! Oh yes…the legacy continues! It's amazing how, in one breath, my son could tell me how mean it was for "HIS OWN MOTHER" to do that to him, and then in the next breath be so energized about doing it to someone else! Ain't that just the way we are?!

You know, just thinking about it, I'm slightly embarrassed to say I've been on MANY "snipe" hunts. I have found myself waiting for something to come along that never did…all the while being bewildered and looking terribly stupid…with sack in hand. Well, I made it back to the house every time and have probably been "the better" for it. A snipe hunt every once in a while is good for the soul. Kinda makes you realize you ain't got it all together like you thought you did! Okay, lighten up… it's only proof that you and I are official card carriers of the human race. So when you find yourself getting too overtaken by something that's not gonna amount to a hill of beans ten years from now, take a good look around you. Is that a sack I see in your hands? Snipe, anyone?

Colt Wrangler and his sidekick, Gunner

THE GENTLE GIANT

I remember the day we bought him. It was at a local farm sale. We knew the people, and my mother was sent to the sale specifically for the purpose of buying him. Dad had given my mother strict instructions as to how much to bid on him and no more! He was a red roan, draft-bred stallion (we called them strawberry roans back then). He was huge… raised by six kids, and he adored children. My dad needed him to skid logs off the wooded hillsides. His name was Prince. As the bidding on Prince began, all six kids gathered around mom (kids can always recognize a softy). When she reached her "limit" and the bids kept going up, all six kids began begging, tugging on momma's clothes and looking up at her with big crocodile tears in their eyes. Well, you know what she did. We came home with Prince.

You know, I don't remember what we paid for him, but whatever it was… it wasn't near what he was worth. I was way too small to bridle or saddle him, but I would run hay baling twine through his halter, lead him up to something I could climb up on, crawl over on Prince, and off we'd go. We'd head across the fields at a lope; I'd eventually bounce off, and Prince would stop and wait until I could get him up against something and get back on, and off we'd go again.

I think sometimes God just drops something "other than"…something special in an animal and personally shapes them for us Himself, and through that animal, God <u>plays</u> with us…delighting in us. Problem is, we can too easily get our eyes totally on the animal and never regard the One Who MADE him for us because He LOVES us! We SHOULD care for our animals. Proverbs says a kind man regards the life of his beast; but there's a need to look further than the animal. Look to the One Who created all things, and as you begin to know the Creator, you will love and appreciate all of creation on a more balanced scale.

These days a weird thing is happening. The same people who fight to save a whale are the ones who fight for the right to kill an unborn child! Should we love and regard life, animals, and nature in general? You bet!

But not to know the Creator of it all is to begin to worship the creation MORE than the Creator Himself. When that happens, animals start being more important in our estimation than humans. If you've ever wondered whether or not God has even cared…He cared enough to send His own Son to be brutalized at our hands for our own salvation. He was so intimately involved with your pain as a child that when He saw you cry, He caused that special pet to lick the tears from your face. When He can't touch us through a human, He'll touch us through an animal. But the point is…He is the One Who has sent HIS love into the earth to us! What a shame it is to regard our animals with a warm heart and never give adequate recognition and allegiance to the One Who CREATED them!

I think back at Prince and realize how God watched over me through that horse. A literal four-legged guardian angel. To this day Prince holds a special place in my memory, and since that time, I have come to know, love, trust, and appreciate the One Who MADE him just for me!

Riding with Tyger in the Smokey Mountains during a short time off while stationed at Fort Bragg, NC

WAGON WHEEL PHILOSOPHY

Have you ever noticed how your life runs in cycles? Kinda like a wagon wheel. Sometimes you're on top, and sometimes you're on the bottom. Good news is, when you're down, you won't stay there as long as you keep going forward. Stop there and it's all over, but as long as you keep moving forward, you WILL be out of the mud hole. Bad news is, if you're on top...oh well, we don't have to go there.

Everything cycles. The earth cycles, seasons cycle, the moon cycles, the economy cycles...everything that is alive cycles. We love to talk about those times when we were on top...shining...but it's the low times that make or break a person. Character is built not by successes but by struggles. Every truly great person I can think of had to go through some really tough times to become the person they had to be, to do the things they did. Therefore, it really wasn't what they DID that was as important as who they BECAME.

People have done some incredible things that changed the course of history; for that, we should be eternally grateful, but I am convinced that God is more interested in who we become than in what we do. He can pay a man's taxes through a fish and speak to an obstinate prophet through the mouth of a donkey...God can DO something through anything just fine. God ***using me*** is not a problem. God has used some mighty shady characters to get His work done! But when it comes to who we BECOME, now that's where God's hands are sometimes tied. Our will must agree, or God cannot work.

That's where the cycles come in. Everyone and everything goes through them, and what or who we become as a result of those cycles is often up to us. The Bible says a righteous man falls seven times and gets back up. It's not the falling that's the problem...it's the refusal to get up again that buries a person. Cycles are just a part of life, and what we do when we go through them determine who we become in the end. Some of the best things that ever happened to me are things I hope to God I never have to go through ever again. Looking back, though, it's easy to see that the adjustments in character that came as a result of what I went through were greatly needed.

We desperately need to get it through our thick heads that God isn't as interested in what we <u>do</u> FOR Him as He is in who we <u>become</u> IN Him. If we ever catch on to this truth, we'll stop trying to get delivered out of our circumstances and, instead, start allowing God to work on <u>US</u> while we're IN THEM. Knowing this…that our circumstances WILL CHANGE as long as we move forward.

Maybe your wagon wheel is just about to make its upward turn? Hang on, baby! Better times are coming! Let's just pray we all become better PEOPLE in the process!

Colt riding in the Grand Entry with me at Manawa, WI

BARE-ING ALL

It was one of those memorable moments. I was singing horseback at a PRCA rodeo in East Texas. It was the very first year I had ever done such a thing. Tyger was about five, and Colt was closing in on two. We had older kids watching ours and had given them strict instructions to keep the door on the bus locked so that the younger ones couldn't get out while I was singing. Thirty minutes…that's all we needed.

All was going along nicely. I'm in the middle of the concert when, horror of horrors, crawling through the pipe arena fence and heading straight for me is Colt Wrangler. Within fifteen minutes time, Colt had gotten out the door undetected and was heading for the sound of Momma's voice as fast as his little legs could carry him. Did I mention he was naked as a plucked bird? That's right, he had taken advantage of the situation and removed his diaper along the way; it made for faster mobility you know. Dragging his beloved "blankie" in the dirt behind him, here he came, wearing nothing but a smile! He was a showstopper, for sure. All I could do was stop singing, dismount, and introduce my son while the crowd was applauding and thoroughly enjoying the candid camera moment. Colt was delighted as he had found "Mommy" and came walking with his little arms extended, requesting to be picked up and held. Hold him I did as I carried my precious one, leading the horse out the arena.

Isn't that a picture of how we should be with God? No matter what's going on around us, we head for the sound of Daddy's voice, determined to work our way through whatever obstacles we might encounter along the way. Being naked and vulnerable before God will cause Him to stop in His tracks and pick us up in His arms. Wouldn't it be wonderfully freeing if we could be that way no matter who was watching, caring nothing about what anyone else thought of us? No wonder the Lord said that we must approach Him as a child. The moment I saw Colt Wrangler walking naked into the arena holding his little arms out to me, I was smitten. At that moment, nothing was as important as holding my son in my arms. The concert wasn't important anymore. What anyone thought wasn't important. Finishing the song wasn't important. The thing I wanted to do most was hold my son. Got the picture? That's just a tiny fraction of how God feels towards us as we approach Him with nothing hidden, no pretenses, just naked honesty. Try seeking Him out, He's not hard to find…you were made to be held by the Father.

COURAGE THAT INSPIRES

In rodeo as well as any sport, it's about heart. It's not always the most talented that wins the prize; sometimes it's simply the one with the most heart, the one who is willing to risk all, the one who just won't quit. The great racehorse Seabiscuit was the epitome of heart. He outran horses twice his size at lengths that were more suited to his opponents than himself. He had heart. He was willing to bare all. He gave EVERYTHING…every time.

It's that kind of attitude that sports are built upon. It's that kind of heart that glues us to the TV to see a guy go the distance when mediocrity would have long ago thrown in the towel. Something about it challenges us to go further, try harder, dig deeper. We get inspired when we see someone have the courage to throw caution to the wind and dare to give all for what they believe can be done. It's that type of courage and heart that birthed this nation, and it's what shaped our nation for greatness in its beginning. It's that kind of heart that a competitor is looking for in a horse. That kind is rare, and you can't tell what's there by looking at the outside; it's hidden within the heart and isn't revealed until put to the test.

Why are we so inspired by heart and inner fortitude? God designed us this way. This is exactly what God is looking for in His children, an inner passion that fuels a strength that's beyond natural ability. God delights in empowering His kids, but He has to have something to empower! He can't empower passivity, complacency, or self-preservation. If you're looking for an "easy religion," Christianity isn't it. Not biblical Christianity anyway. True biblical Christianity is not for the weak of heart. God is looking for some leaders He can partner with in the arena of life that won't quit and lose heart the first time they encounter some bumps and bruises along the way. You could be who God is looking for!

When the prophet Samuel was sent to anoint one of Jesse's boys to be the next king of Israel. When Samuel looked at David's older brothers, he thought, "Surely this is the next king," but God spoke right back and told Samuel it's not what he looks like on the outside but what he is on the INSIDE that counts. God went on to say, "I have refused him."

David's older brothers had the chance to be anointed for the task but failed to have that "extra something" on the inside that God was looking for. Later on, it showed up under pressure, as it always does. When Goliath stepped out on the field and gave his challenge, David answered while his older brothers cowered in fear with the ranks of Israel.

David had heart. It's the kind of "risk-all attitude" for something greater than a normal existence that God is looking for! You can be the one God is looking for to show Himself strong to. As the scripture says, His eyes are searching over the whole earth for that "one"…the one who dares to live by a courageous heart while others are caving in under pressure. Do you…can you…dare to be that one?

Photo shoot with my handsome man!!
He's just so cool and so much FUN.

WINNING THE RACE

I was watching *Seabiscuit* the other day; I hadn't watched it in a long time. When I got to the part where he lost the race at Santa Anita, California, it spoke volumes to me. I didn't even finish the movie. I turned it off…God was talking.

During the race, Red was fouled and became so angry that he set out to get the other jockey back. He became obsessed with simply beating the other guy…as a result he lost the race. After the race, both the owner and the trainer of Seabiscuit were asking Red why he didn't follow the game plan that would have ensured a first place win. His response was that he had been fouled. When they looked blankly at him, he just got louder…"they fouled me…they FOULED ME!!!" When Red Pollard asked if they expected him to simply do *nothing* about the foul, their reply was…YES!! He was so angry over being fouled he couldn't understand their thinking.

I can relate. God says to me, "Why are you sitting here in the ditch?"…and I look up horrified and reply, "Didn't You see that, God? I got FOULED!" I become so absorbed over a wrong done to me and wanting that incident immediately made right that I lost sight of the REAL issue, which is finishing the race.

The best way for Red to have been exonerated was to keep to the game plan and WIN! So it is with us. God has a "game plan," if I may call it so, and if we stick to HIS ways…His methods…His directives… we WILL win, PERIOD. In this life's race, we ALL get fouled. The trick is not to allow that offense to get us so distracted that we lose sight of our future. Some fouls are powerful enough to bump us smooth out of the race if we allow it. The really cool thing about all this is…no one…and I mean NO ONE, can take you out of the race without your permission! If you and I will simply choose to let the offense go…release it…forgive the offending one, we immediately are back on track. Many people have a wrong idea of what forgiveness actually is. They think it means that we're saying what was done was "okay." It's not that. Not even close.

Forgiveness simply releases the offender from our hands into God's. It wasn't Red's place to judge the race…his was to run. So it is with us. I am not the Judge. Whenever I try to be, I forfeit my place in the race. The smartest thing to do is to let the foul go and focus on finishing well! Holding unforgiveness will disqualify us probably faster than anything else. It holds us in the past, keeps us tormented, and altogether takes us out of the running. It's simply not worth it. Keep your focus true…let God handle the rest.

Precious time spent with my sons!

BARROOM MIRACLES

Some days, the strangest opportunities present themselves to you. This was one of those times. A call came into my office asking if I'd be willing to come and sing Christian music in a bar located in a small Texas town. It seemed the owner of the bar was being moved upon by God, and when these things happen, strange opportunities arise. One evening during the week, he had strippers come as entertainment, and for whatever reason (heavenly inspired insanity?), he wanted another evening for an hour of gospel music. I guess he was attempting to create an "all-purpose bar"?? I wasn't about to pass up such a weird opportunity!

I got there, and it was a very cool-looking bar on the inside with the front end of an old pickup mounted on the wall behind the stage that faced the bar, along with an open area of tables and chairs and a balcony up above, large enough for several pool tables.

I only had soundtracks to sing with, and everyone knows that is simply NOT COOL. Oh how I wished I had a live band to back me up so as to impress and entertain, but nope…just me…on stage…no horse, nothing cool to use to engage this group of people who already hated me. Don't misunderstand me, I KNEW what to expect when I agreed to come. I KNEW they would consider me as "the church lady" who was coming with her tambourine to sing old gospel hymns. So, as expected, everyone had their backs to me as they drank and succeeded in ignoring me completely. The balcony above was alive with guys busy playing pool and loudly talking, laughing, and just generally having a good time. The atmosphere in the place was one of…"I hate her, but I can ignore her for an hour, and she'll leave and we'll have our bar back."

I remember having cotton mouth so bad as I sang! The atmosphere was THICK with opposition. But this is when the unexpected happened. Just barely into the second song, a WIND came through the building. Now, with no doors open and no windows, this wasn't possible…but yet, it happened. I thought since it was a supernatural occurrence, that I was the only one feeling it, but that wasn't the case. Every person sitting at the bar set down their drinks, spun around on the bar stools, quit visiting, and faced me. The bartender, barmaids, everyone seated at the tables stopped talking and were held captive in their focus. And what REALLY amazed me was how ALL the guys playing pool in the balcony INSTANTLY stopped playing, laid their pool sticks on the tables, and leaned over the balcony, and for the next hour, the entire place didn't stir while I mostly sang but also shared along the way!

I wish I could say I sang "that good," but honestly…NO ONE SINGS THAT GOOD!!! This was totally supernatural and God's doing! I have since learned that when a heavenly wind blows through a place, it's the effect of angels sent there to change the atmosphere, making it conducive to people's hearts becoming open and softened to receive a touch from their Maker. As long as I live, I will never forget that night! I ended it in prayer with people all over the bar praying out loud, placing their hearts and lives into the hands of a loving Savior. When my hour was up, I spent another hour visiting with people, and as sound equipment was being loaded back into the trailer, they were still following us out into the parking lot!

I have learned that if we will answer opportunities presented to us that place us in precarious environments far exceeding our abilities, God will often step in and do something spectacular! Oh, how He looks for people of passion, willing to step out in courage wherever He leads! Sometimes true faith is spelled R-I-S-K.

HOG-RIDING MEMORIES

Kids are great. There's so much you can do with them that's totally entertaining. When Colt Wrangler was about four, we had a pet hog. Her name was Porkchop. One day I had this brilliant idea to put this tiny saddle we had on her…just to see what she'd do. She didn't even seem to notice…so we upped the experience. We called for Colt Wrangler. That's what kids are for…right?

"Wanna ride Porkchop, Colt?"

"Sure!"

We placed him in the saddle…kinda sloping downhill, forward like, told him to keep his feet in front of him and hang on tight! Nothing happened. Porkchop just grunted at all this attention. Soooo I went to get some incentive…cat food. Porkchop LOVED dry cat food. (What is it with cat food? EVERYTHING likes it!) I put some cat food in a coffee can, walked out ahead of Porkchop, and shook the can. She bolted like a racehorse out of the gates. I took off running with Porkchop chasing me and squealing the whole way. Colt's head snapped back in a sort of whiplash fashion, but he remained in the saddle…for a while…then off he bounced to one side. He hit the ground laughing.

"Do it again, Momma…do it again!"

I'd pour Porkchop some cat food on the ground, remount Colt, walk quietly off a distance, and shake the can again. The whole scenario was repeated.

"Faster, Momma…**faster**!" (I don't know why he was wanting more speed. He wasn't staying on as it was!)

I tell you, it was hilarious!! I wish we had had a video camera!

One night I watched as Colt Wrangler set his bronc saddle on the spur board, lifted the bronc rein, and worked his feet. My, my, how they grow…wasn't it just yesterday he was "setting his feet" on a pet pig? Of all the times we've had with our kids, I now wish I would have left the dirty dishes, or whatever I thought was "so important" at the time, and played more. I've noticed that the kids' favorite memories are not the things that we bought them, but the EXPERIENCES WE SHARED WITH THEM. Why do we have to grow old before we begin to fully recognize what's important?

I'm beginning to recognize, too, that our Father God is the same way. He'd rather we spend time with Him than simply "do our duty" where He is concerned. He wants more than a bored hour on Sunday morning and a "tip" thrown into the plate to appease Him…or is it to appease our guilt? Whichever. The fact is, that Jesus is God, Who came to earth in a human body simply because He wants to build a relationship with YOU. Relationships are only built by sharing experiences, building trust, listening, and opening up our hearts. The more we do that with our kids, the stronger our relationship with them becomes. The same is true with Jesus. Take some time this week to build those relationships. I can promise…you will create some great memories along the way.

Colt Wrangler on Porkchop, 1995

Killed Hopes and Dead Chickens

The year was 1989. We were driving home from Cheyenne Frontier Days where Ray missed winning the second go-round and going into the short-go in the bull riding by 6/10th of a second. Not much was spoken that LONG trip back to Arkansas where we were living at the time. I couldn't understand why. We desperately needed the money, and the $4,400 or so for winning the round at that time would have made all the difference in the world for us. I tried but couldn't completely hold back the tears. To make matters worse, when we finally pulled onto our little rented farm two days later, the entire place was littered with dead chickens. Every chicken we had was dead. Our neighbor's hounds had gotten loose and had a field day. No one bothered to come clean up after the slaughter, and chickens that had been lying dead in the July heat for three days or so were rotting everywhere…even on our front porch. That took care of our yearly harvest of chickens for the freezer. Once I got over the immediate surge of anger, I cried again.

We unloaded the truck, stepping over and around chicken corpses, went into the house, and checked the phone messages. That's when we first heard about Lane Frost getting killed in the short-go at Cheyenne. At first, I just didn't believe it. We had just seen Lane that Saturday. Surely this was a cruel, cruel joke. Once the truth soaked in, I cried more.

What's up with these times in our lives? I sure can't say with any confidence that I know, but one thing I have learned is this…when you have a series of crushing blows, know for a certainty that the enemy of your soul is seeking to take you out. Oh, he may not be trying to kill you, he just wants to stop your forward movement. If he can get you to cave in, stop pressing forward, quit believing, lose your courage, stop caring…you might as well be dead. You see, sometimes the devil isn't so much after YOU as he is after your destiny!

Something else about that summer at Cheyenne; Marty Staneart covered the bull "Mr. T." Mr. T had gone unridden for five years at 188 attempts. Marty was the first man ever to cover him, but instead of his accomplishment being the "big event" that year, understandably, Lane's death overshadowed everything. How often do we allow a "death" of something to cast its shadow over the good, and instead of focusing on the joy of what is, we settle into grieving over what isn't.

What is it in your life you can find JOY in? What is there that you can truly thank God over? It's there…. you may have to step around a few things that died, but it's there…find it. Take your focus off the loss and place it on the God Who can lead you into greater possibilities. Look at what's staring you in the face that's GOOD. Begin to defeat the spirit of death by the sheer effort of praising Him for His goodness toward you. God has GOOD plans for you…plans to give you hope and a future (Jeremiah 29:11). Make a choice to not be defeated by trying circumstances and hard times. You can make it through today. Leave tomorrow in God's hands. Clean the "dead things" out of your life, and make room for God again. Hope always returns when a place has been made for it.

Moving cows at the base of the Prior Mountains in MT

AM I A LOOSE HORSE?

The other day, I did a picture sermon using my stallion, Strider.

After riding around in the arena and singing a couple of songs, I got off, unsaddled him, and removed his bridle. He did exactly as I expected. He happily trotted off and began to do his "stud-ly ritual"—smelling poop FIRST, rolling in the dirt SECOND, and all in all completely ignoring me. Even though I own Strider—I paid a price to call him mine—he could choose to ignore me in this situation. I asked the crowd, "Is Strider focused on me?" The obvious answer was NO.

We can do the same with God. Some of us have said "yes" to Jesus and become His. But even though He has legal ownership of us by a great and costly price He paid, we can still choose to ignore Him! We can spend our lives smelling poop and rolling in the dirt and not realizing how costly it is to do so. You see, Psalm 34:8 says "Oh TASTE and SEE that the Lord is good." That implies EXPERIENCING HIM!! God doesn't simply want "ownership" of us. He wants us to EXPERIENCE Him!

By moving closer to Strider, I got his attention long enough for him to come to me. I bridled him and led him to the center of the arena. But unless he yielded to my request and laid down, I was helpless to climb aboard. Unlike some of you men, I cannot swing up on a 14-hand horse, much less one that's 16.1! Strider quickly did as I asked, and I got on him. Now…we could move TOGETHER! His talents, training, and strength under my direction could suddenly come alive by being in sync with me. Suddenly what simply was a "loose horse" changed into fluid movement with purpose and beauty! That's EXACTLY like us! We were NEVER created to be NORMAL!! But we can never attain to what God created us for without allowing God to rest His "super on our natural." He wants to "clothe me" in Himself, and in that union, I suddenly become something I cannot be without Him!

God NEVER intended our relationship with Him to be limited to a church service! If all we know of God is through a preacher, then that's second rate AT BEST. We can do our "church thing" and still basically live a life ignoring God. God wants us to TASTE and SEE… EXPERIENCE for ourselves His goodness! We can't do that without yielding to Him and inviting His presence to come rest on us. What a waste to spend our lives basically ignoring the One Who paid such a high price to buy us for Himself! We forfeit a life of supernatural adventures and wonderment when we don't "taste and see."

I can buy a cookbook and memorize its recipes, but unless I cook and EAT the food, I've missed the whole point of the book. Just so, we can memorize scriptures but never go on to EXPERIENCING what those verses are inviting us to experience! A walk with God is a life of experiencing His presence, His supernatural interventions, knowing His voice and His touch and experiencing His abilities placed upon my lack…making me "other than" what I am without Him!

May we all turn from a lower existence of rolling in the dirt and smelling poop to placing our focus on the only One Who can elevate us to a higher life, a life of supernatural guidance and purpose with beauty!

Pushing cows 

BITING DOGS, ANGRY HORSE, AND SCREAMING RIDER

It was a nice workout in a nice indoor arena where all was proceeding "nicely" UNTIL…

My dog Ruger was playing in the dirt and another dog, also named Ruger, a red heeler cross, in his boredom came to "play." As I'm loping between barrels, the heeler mix Ruger ran in under Strider, got stepped on, and as a result, got totally PO'd and started barking and biting Strider's heels! My Ruger happily joined into this apparently FUN game when out of my peripheral vision, I caught sight of him going in for the hind legs. Strider is stomping at one dog on the front end and trying to kick the one behind as it quickly escalated into rearing and leaping and kicking while I'm screaming out the one name of BOTH dogs, who seemingly at this point were totally deaf or had completely FORGOTTEN their names!!

This was NOT how I had foreseen the afternoon ride to go. I actually remember (as I was teetering dangerously off to one side of the saddle) having the thought come to mind, that it's been a LONG TIME since I've felt the impact of being pie-yied like a yard dart off the back of a horse. That alone got my mind to thinking how what I was doing in response to what was happening was NOT WORKING, and I'd better come up with a different approach as how to bring this situation to a more pleasant end! Since the dogs were only getting MORE hyper-oriented, I decided that instead of trying to hold Strider in place, I would push him OUT and make the dogs run! That proved to be the answer, as this quickly discouraged the bull dog from having to run down his quarry. I guess it was fun as long as the prey made itself a meal on his plate, but having to run down his prey?? Naw!! The "other Ruger" quickly gave it up, and all settled back down into a semblance of normality.

Sometimes it's best to change up your response to what's happening around you. If the response you give seems to escalate the situation, if the situation is one where the attitudes are already escalated, did you ever stop to think that adding a higher crescendo into the mix only adds to the escalation of stupidity?? I have slowly come to the realization that stupidity shouted louder than everyone else in the room is STILL stupidity! I've also become aware of the fact that sometimes, not always but sometimes, simply RESPONDING to an atmosphere inundated in stupidity is like taking hold of an anvil when already standing in quicksand. Just being there puts you in danger, but entering in with your mouth is a no-win situation! Retreat quickly and live to fight another day!!

Bottom line: Sometimes you CANNOT bring peace into a situation, and when that's obviously the case, you have no other option but to protect your own inner peace by removing yourself from the arena where the dogs are biting.

Goat-tying days

CHANGING LEADS

If you were drawn to this article in hopes of getting wisdom for training your horse to do flying lead changes, don't waste your time. Turn to someone who knows…and that's certainly NOT me! But there is a principle here that weighs truthful in other areas of life concerning lead changes.

Years ago, I was blessed to breeze racehorses for an older woman who was an encyclopedia of horse knowledge. She insisted that her racehorses be well trained and not just be unbroken colts running fast more from fear than good training. She was adamant that her horses be able to change leads easily so they could better maneuver getting out of a tight spot during a race. And that sometimes, that little bit of knowledge could make the difference between winning or losing.

A few weeks ago, I spent time with a good trainer friend of mine, and he was instructing me on the beginning exercises needed to prepare a horse for learning a smooth flying lead change. He had me doing counter arcs with my horse. You know what that is, right? It's where you lope a circle in one direction while having your horse's head face outward from the circle. In other words, you're loping one direction, but your horse's head is facing another.

We as individuals and also as a nation can get stuck in one lead, and changing that lead is desperately needed for the benefit of our future. Learning to switch leads fluidly and easily to transition from one direction to another is MOST IMPORTANT if we want to finish our race well! And sometimes, when we're NOT getting it, we need to be brought through some exercises where our eyes are turned OUTWARD instead of inward, so as to position us for a much-needed shift in direction!

America as a nation is in a counter arc right now, and it's a GOOD THING because the direction our nation has been traveling in has been uncomfortable, to say the least…the results will prove to be very refreshing! While many people in our nation are upset over this shift, and sad to say, that even includes many who consider themselves Christians, our leadership (the head) is looking outward. Even though that puts the nation in a place of unrest, it's imperative that we be in this counter arc so as to change the entire direction of our nation—from self-imposed destruction to fulfilling the destiny that America was birthed to ultimately fulfill.

These are exciting times, and to be overwrought in fear over all the unrest is to believe that we will be stranded in this counter arc forever. No, the counter arc is NOT the destination…it's the pathway to a much-needed transition and change of direction. This is a matter of necessity for the destiny of our nation and other nations that will follow suit. Whether we realize it or not, we've been "boxed in" for several decades now by those whose agenda is for their own self-interest and NOT for the nation. Maneuvering out of this trap demands we change leads. The difference in winning or losing is at stake…so I say "Thank God for this counter arc America is experiencing!" We're in the process of making a flying lead change! May we as a nation get back on course with the direction GOD has for us, and may we be able to proclaim with confidence, "God bless America"…AGAIN!

Duke

I got a new dog. He's a Dutch Shepherd, two and a half years old. He was on an adoption site, a military dog that flunked out of bomb-sniffing school. His whole life history was one of being on a leash or in a crate, being trained, and handed off to strangers. I drove four hours to meet the man and get Duke. On the trip back, I could tell Duke was a tad concerned as to what turn his life was taking now. I didn't know if he'd warm up to me or simply go nuts with a newfound freedom and run off, but I was NOT going to have a dog who must be tied to stay with me. My first move was to turn him loose on twenty acres that was completely fenced with woven wire and just let him RUN.

Oh my! What a sensory overload this new place must've been to Duke!! He'd NEVER been in the country…only city life. He peed on EVERY bush he smelled until he simply ran dry of pee. He discovered deer…prickly pear…and skunks. I knew that had to happen. At first, he didn't want to come to me. I could understand why. He figured if I got my hands on him, back in confinement he'd go, and he was LOVING this newfound freedom! He didn't want this world to go away…like waking up from a dream of exhilarating freedom and finding yourself back in jail.

The next day I had to drive to town and asked Duke to "load up." He ducked his head and went back to the trailer. I knew what he was thinking…"She's going to take me away and give me to someone else or put me back in a crate." After I loaded him in the truck, ran my errands, came back, and unloaded him, he was ecstatic!

After a few days of this, you could SEE his mind contemplating the whole deal. "Maybe this IS my life now! Maybe SHE is the center of this new life. Maybe this WON'T end, and I can relax and trust her and be loyal to her as my life's source."

We've only had a week together at this point, but Duke is already showing great loyalty to me. And happy????? Oh my gosh, he's happy!! His face has a whole new expression on it. But every once in a while, something will trigger him, and he'll have a sudden reaction to something that caused old memories and fears to rush back in. He's afraid of losing freedom. It's not that he minds being tied up. That still has to happen. It's a fear of all this GOOD, ending!

Duke is learning to trust my character…I'm good…I will NEVER want him harmed. My desire toward him is ALWAYS for his own benefit. All I expect back from Duke is his loyalty. I just want to enjoy him and let him enjoy being with me. I don't want a dog that must be on a leash to stay with me. I want his love. This is TOTALLY, COMPLETELY, AND EXACTLY what the Lord wants of US!! God is GOOD! He will NEVER desire you harm, and ALWAYS His desire is for your benefit! All He asks is we learn to TRUST HIM and become LOYAL in our relationship. And God doesn't give up on us or throw us away! Our place in Him is SECURE!

Wow…the things you can learn from a dog.

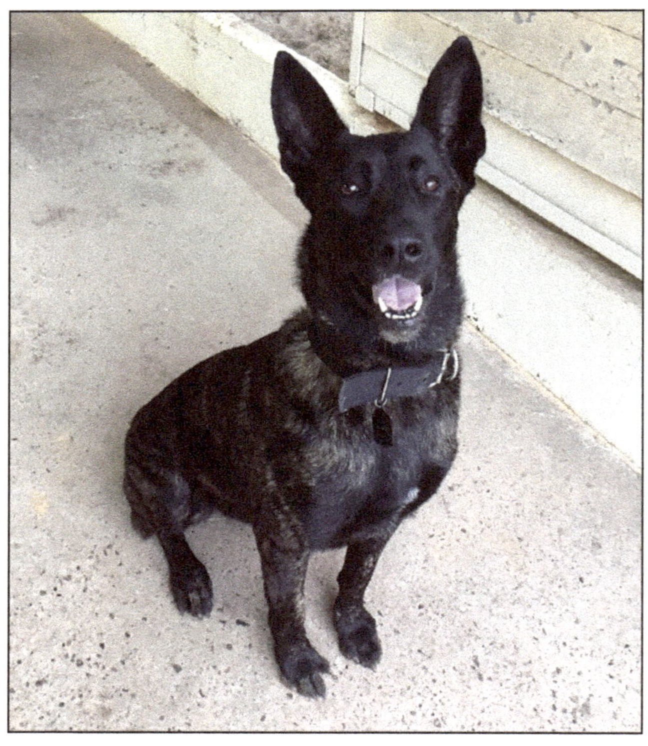

Duke, my HAPPY Dutch Shepherd 2018

IN THE ARMS OF COMPASSION

I have on my lap, at the moment I am writing this article, a kitten that had been dumped and obviously starved for quite some time. I pulled up at a fuel station last night and happened to see him limping slowly to hide under some plastic milk crates. My heart went out to him, and with a bit of food, I got him caught. He stunk horribly. He was so weak and frail he could barely get around, and his entire back end was plastered in his own poop. He was so very glad to be rescued that even while bathing him, he purred the entire time!

This morning, as I wrapped him in a towel after his second bath and carried him in my arms while starting the truck, I thought he might freak out a bit. The noise of a huge diesel engine and doors shutting obviously made him a little ill at ease, but he never tried to get out of my arms. It was then that I felt the Lord was talking to me through this raggedy kitten.

I've been feeling pretty rotten lately. Disappointed within myself at the level I'm operating in. I'm also a tad frustrated with the "holding pattern" it seems I've been in for years. I know within myself that God has SO MUCH MORE for me to step into, but NOTHING has seemed to change in my life for several years now. I'm HUNGRY for more. I feel extremely weak and powerless to change ANYTHING in my life. Does ANY of this resonate with you?

The Lord used a mostly starved, flea-infested, filthy, helpless kitten to give me a PICTURE of Who He is. He impressed upon me that this kitten was totally helpless to change his circumstances, and by the horrible shape his little body was in, it was easy to see he had been existing in this situation for quite some time. But in ONE MOMENT, his life took a complete change of direction! Not from anything he did. There was nothing beautiful about him to attract me to him. He had nothing to offer me but his problems. I already HAVE a cat on the road with me…I do NOT need another cat! Sooooo why did I rescue him? Compassion.

It's the same with you and me. I don't have ANYTHING to offer God but my screwups, my weaknesses, my issues, my need…just me… fleas and all. As I carried that tiny bag of bones in my arms, he had NO INTENTION of jumping out, and the Lord spoke to my heart and said, "I want you to trust me like this kitten is trusting you. He has no idea where you're taking him and he doesn't CARE, because you are LIFE to him and he TRUSTS you! He has found a place of REST in your arms…you're his source, his security, his quality of life. Be like this kitten and realize that's what I AM to you. Let Me carry you wherever I choose and trust My timing."

Oh, and just as his life dragged on without ANY HOPE of change and seemingly no kindness offered from anyone, in ONE MOMENT, he went from near death to life!

God KNOWS where you are!

You and I don't need to earn His love or impress Him with our actions. He just LOVES us…because that's Who He IS! He's COMPASSION. Let Him "catch you" and simply trust Him as He carries you in the direction HE knows is perfect for you!

Colt Wrangler always had a "good seat and balance" about him!

Omgosh! Am I a Socialist?

I entered my FIRST horse show with Strider just the other day. That's right…this dyed-in-the-wool, rodeo-oriented, horse-show-hating cowgirl fell so low as to actually ENTER a horse show! Now, before any horse show people throw this story into the bottom of a bird cage, hear me out!!

My Gypsy Vanner stallion needs some exposure beyond the world of rodeo where he's simply a unique piece of God's handiwork in creating beautiful horses. So between events, I was able to slide into Sedalia for the Missouri State Fair. Not knowing anything about what I was getting myself into, I only entered one class: Trail. I figured Strider being well broke and not afraid of anything…except for charging buffalo…(he had that happen to him once and was WISE enough to get out of Dodge!) that we were SAFE with that class.

Show day arrived, and after a trial run through the pattern, Strider aced it! He did a perfect 360-degree turn inside a tiny square, side passed up to a mailbox, crossed over a bridge and over logs, never touching a one. He hit his right leads flawlessly and even bowed at the end, to the crowd's delight…only to find out we were disqualified because I rode with a snaffle bit. It never occurred to me that I should read the rules!

But to my utter delight, I found the horse show people to be some of THE FUNNEST folks I've been around in a while! And let me tell you…I travel around FUN people! They literally babysat me and Strider, and when the day ended, I was invited to eat supper with a large group of Gypsy Vanner people. At the supper table, I popped off to them that they should all pitch in and give me some of the extra ribbons they'd won that day so I could go home and tell my friends that Strider was SO AWESOME…he had won ALL those ribbons in a single class! They all laughed, and the conversation remained lighthearted all evening. The next morning, almost everyone had cleared out soon after daybreak, and when I went to feed Strider, I was met with ribbons hung all over his stall door. I laughed so hard at those crazy, awesome folks who had the "last laugh" on me!

There was one first place, one second, three thirds, and a fourth-place ribbon hung on his stall! It wasn't 'til a few days later it hit me…that was a picture of what liberals like to call "spreading the wealth." The hard work, good performance, and investment it took for those contestants to win those ribbons was handed over to somebody who actually didn't care about ribbons and wasn't interested enough to even read the rules! Nor was I willing to put out the effort all those folks had put out to excel in their field! Socialism at its simplest! What someone else earns with hard work is handed over to others who DON'T!! They did it out of jest and because of a new friendship. But in reality…that's why socialism has NEVER WORKED, nor will it ever work in the future. Why excel if EVERYONE gets a ribbon?? Why work hard if your hard work is going to be given to someone who doesn't care enough to work at all?

I've kept those ribbons. Not because I give them any value in themselves, but because of a newfound friendship with some totally WONDERFUL people in the horse show world!!

Strider's stall in Sedalia, MO 2017

Shank Him!

Stallions…don't ya just LOVE dealing with them??!! A friend told me this story on her husband, and you KNOW how us cowgirl-type people just LOVE IT when we get something over on our men!! She had this big black stud, and she was leading him out to live cover a mare. He was getting ahead of her as she struggled to get him under control. Instead of coming to her aid, her husband just kept yelling, "Shank him…SHANK HIM!"

If you've been in a similar situation, you KNOW how aggravating it is to have someone yelling instructions from the sidelines when it's taking everything you've got just to keep your legs underneath you! Her time came to get even when her husband was leading said stallion out for another breeding. He tripped, and as he was being drug on his belly across the gravel, instead of stepping in to aid him…sporting a sort of triumphant smirk…she simply yelled, "Shank him…SHANK HIM!" I can type out this story, but to hear her tell it had us all doubling over in laughter. She passed into heaven a few years back, and this story as well as others were told at her graduation as we celebrated her life with plenty of tears and much laughter.

The other day I got a call to collect Strider for a mare in another state.

Since I'm rarely in the same place when I get those calls, I don't have the convenience of the vets knowing my stud. One of the places I went, the vet asked if I wanted him to handle Strider, and I said definitely YES and explained that he isn't mean, but he's VERY STRONG. When I saw the setup, I was a bit more concerned as there was NOTHING between the mounting dummy and the mare. Then I found out…there wasn't even a mare! They had a gelding they were going to use. As they were getting ready to lead Strider out there, I suggested that the gelding not be positioned as they had him…directly in front of Strider…but to move him to where the mounting dummy was between Strider and the gelding. The young vet quickly told me that he was going to lead Strider at an arc as that's how he like doing it. So I apologized for butting in and backed off.

Enter vet and stallion: Problem was…that arc thing the vet had in mind didn't cross Strider's mind at all, and as soon as they came around the building, Strider aimed for the only horse he saw. The vet fell down and was dragging on his belly across the grass. The girl holding the poor unsuspecting gelding never moved until the vet started yelling, "MOVE!" I added an adjective and yelled "FAST!!!" I was releasing the name of Jesus over the entire situation as SOMETIMES there simply isn't enough time to fashion a proper prayer. In those times, I've learned that saying "JESUS!" kinda covers it all! It worked, thank God! Because instead of Strider being in his typical "butt whooping mood," he had no desire to hurt that gelding and started smelling horse poop instead. Girl and gelding got safely away, as did the vet, though his pride may have been a tad wounded.

All in all, semen got collected, and I swear I heard my friend speaking from that great crowd of witnesses in heaven, "Shank him… SHANK HIM!" as I drove away with a smile.

**Lady rough stock riders posing for a
picture behind the chutes 1986**

Rodeoing has blessed me to meet some of the
coolest and most talented people over the years!

Destined for Greatness

There comes a time when we all must stand or fall, stay steady, or flip out and look for a more comfortable place to hold up while others withstand the storm that we seek to evade. We all cheer for the person or horse that wins against what looks like impossible odds. We love the heart of a champion, and we ALL want to identify with such, but it takes more than "want to" to align with that image. The one who conquers when all looks lost, pulling a victory out of defeat, is the one who has the stoutness of heart to keep going when nothing spurs a person on but sheer desire and an absolute hatred of the thought of quitting.

I love the war stories of those who never wavered in the face of incredible hardships and won a great victory. I cannot watch the great races of Secretariat or Seabiscuit without tears running out of my eyes as they cross the finish line. Such incredible heart!! I LOVE it!! I am inspired by these incredible feats. But then I ask myself the question… do I have what it takes?

If in my life I am called upon to run my race without falling back when things get tough, can I be counted on not to quit? Or just as bad… go through the motions of finishing but withholding the passion and the courage and the energy that it would take to GIVE ALL for the outcome! Do I have what it takes? I honestly don't know.

But I DO KNOW that IF I call upon the power of God to rise up inside me so as to never fail Him in what He expects of me…I will have what's needed to finish well. Our lives are sorta like sailboats with beautiful sails. We each have our talents, our strengths, and giftings, like the sails on a sailboat. But these sails, no matter how colorful and brightly beautiful they are, are incomplete without the WIND! My gifts and talents are INCOMPLETE without merging with the wind of God! I may look stately while moored in a harbor, but a boat's purpose is not to be safely docked…its purpose is to challenge the waters by engaging the wind!

I believe that the days ahead will reveal some of history's greatest champions, "the people who KNOW their God shall be strong and do great exploits" (Daniel 11:32). In a culture where being kept comfortable is honored above becoming strong, courageous, and inspiring…there will be those who shake off the attitudes of mediocrity, and they will arise to become what God destined them to be in this hour!

One of my favorite lines in *Robin Hood* is "Cometh the times, cometh the man." God has ALWAYS had His champions! If we so desire to BE who God destined us to be, we will be empowered to be His champions for "such a time as this." It starts in the small things. If I am compromising in the small…I CERTAINLY will not stand honorable in the great! Be faithful in the small. Be honorable in the little things. Give encouragement to others even when your heart is heavy. Choose the path of those before us who inspire us to rise above the cowardice of the masses and BECOME that one who makes a difference! Only God knows, but you could be destined for GREATNESS!

Strider…can he be any more handsome?

Two Cultures Colliding

Lately I was back in Colorado, and while there, I totally enjoy the bike trails that run beside the rodeo arenas. I use them to get out in the fresh air, ride my bike while praying, and allow my dog the exercise he needs because of having to be tied at the trailer. I try to pick times where people aren't normally using the trails…well, because I break the rules!! I do good just to ride the bike, but to ADD keeping a dog on a leash who's not USED to being on a leash is an inevitable wreck! Besides that, he doesn't NEED to be on a leash. He stays right with me and doesn't bother other people or their dogs. So off we go…happy…however rebellious!

Last time we went out, we were met with snooty looks and gruff remarks from two separate guys meeting us on bikes. Though I greeted them with a smile and a friendly "good morning" and Ruger was right beside me, away from them and off the trail, they responded gruffly, citing the leash law. That's when it hit me: "Two cultures colliding!" MY world is from a ranching culture, and dogs are NOT on leashes because they don't NEED to be. THEIR world is a world with thousands of people crowded together, and dogs are without freedom or jobs and leashes are a MUST. I understand both sides. That's not the issue. The issue is the disdain that BOTH sides have toward the other. My dog running free… though in NO WAY hindering them…OFFENDS them. Them demanding that my dog be on a leash as if he can't be controlled OFFENDS me. When two opposing cultures collide, two ways of living and thinking OFFENDS what we are familiar with.

Please don't start a debate about me breaking a leash law; the whole point of this isn't "to leash or not to leash," it's the analogy about two cultures colliding. Cultures can collide in all sorts of ways. I have participated in ministry at times when there's hunger for MORE of God. At such times, I will open the door to experience the baptism of the Holy Spirit, and many of them will begin speaking in tongues. This INEVITABLY causes some to get OFFENDED. Why? Because two cultures just collided! Kingdom culture collided with religious culture.

Bumping into something that runs opposite with our familiar belief system always rattles our cages! Even though I know this, it still amazes me how religious thinking wants to keep people on a "leash." When freedom is being experienced and there's great joy in those receiving it, those who DON'T WANT IT always seem to get angry. But there are also those who are more honorable, and though they've never seen anything like that before, they often recognize it's GOD and begin to weigh their options.

Just like I would have to CHOOSE to change my thinking as well as my lifestyle if I wanted city life, if I want to go higher with God, there will be belief systems that must change! If I choose NOT to change, then I remain where I am. Every time God calls me higher, it offends something in me that I'm familiar with and I have a choice to make. If I want to go higher, it will always cost something that must be left behind. In all aspects of life, my choices reveal the culture I prefer.

Going to Sonic in a 2-ton…why not?

WHITE GIRL CAN'T JUMP

My stallion is 16.1 hands; now that's not that tall, but without bringing age into the equation, I simply cannot leap up onto a horse that height! Never could actually. Fact is, this white girl can't jump!! My most energetic efforts get me a few miserably embarrassing inches off the ground. SO when I want to ride Strider bareback, I find a truck tailgate, 4-wheeler, anything I can use to get up on his back. But what if I was in a pinch and there wasn't anything around to rescue my non-athletically jumping self off the ground? Well, I tapped into the answer for that the other day.

A very good horse trainer friend of mine, Dan Grunewald from Helenville, Wisconsin, taught Strider to lay down when I first brought him my horse to train. Dan's opinion (and I very much agree) is when he gets a stallion in, he first settles the issue of who's boss by laying the horse down. As any horse person knows, for a horse to be off his legs is a place of total vulnerability. For a STALLION to be off his legs is extremely humbling, and to be TAUGHT to lay at the feet of a person is being submissive as well as extremely trusting.

I had plenty of board fence to use to mount Strider, but just for grins, I decided to ask him to lay down so I could get on him bareback. He did… and I did. Though it's a simple thing, I was ecstatic over my new mounting experience. Then as I rode off, I had this profound thought. (Yes…they DO occasionally come to me!) I thought of how immensely HUGE God is in proportion to humanity. And how we NEED to be carried by Him, but yet in ourselves, we have ZERO POWER to attain the place where God is.

So GOD had to LOWER Himself! God came to humanity and made Himself so low that anyone, anywhere, at any level of sin-filled existence, could be picked up by Him. HE humbled Himself to come low enough to make Himself accessible to ALL who will humble themselves and reach out to the One Who alone can pick them up from where they are and carry them to where they're supposed to be!

Yeah, I'm a white girl who seriously can't jump, but in this analogy of where God stands to where we are…you can't jump either! Nobody can. Jesus is the full expression of God the Father, Who came in human flesh, lowering Himself to such a place as to be able to carry the entire WORLD. If you will reach out, He will pick you up and carry YOU. He's in love with the human race and more than willing to be your Savior, your Protector, and Provider. He's done His part. He's just waiting for us to meet Him where He is and climb on!

Me and my bud Strider

You Can't Outgive God

We were opening up new territory for church services at pro rodeos that previously hadn't had cowboy church in the mornings of their Sunday performances. Ray had been entering the bull riding at these rodeos for a few years, and we asked the rodeo committee if we could simply have church in the stands. They gladly allowed us that privilege, and little did we know that it would continue for a couple of decades. At some of these rodeos, people would start finding their way into the grand stands an hour before each performance, and this gave us an idea. I offered to sing horseback for free as entertainment for the people arriving early. We figured this would be great advertisement for Sunday morning, as the announcer would advertise the church service at the end of the concert. It worked great, and a service that began with twelve people grew to several hundred fairly quickly.

Problem was, after years of doing this, I began to cop an attitude over doing so much for free and never getting anything more than a rare "thank you" from the committee. After a few years, I gotta say I'd had it. My attitude sucked. I had lost sight of the reason for offering it in the first place. Some years the contract acts would be great, but some years they were pitiful. Knowing that they were getting paid a few hundred dollars for each performance and I was still doing every performance for free, it really chapped my hide.

I remember leaving that rodeo thinking I didn't want to go back, and even worse, I was actually ticked off enough to consider not doing the next rodeo that following weekend for the same reason. Thankfully, I figured I'd better keep my word and show up, but my attitude was…"Bless God, this was gonna be my last year to put out all this effort for free!"

I'd been saving money for my own horse, as I was singing off horses borrowed at each rodeo, and all I had saved was $800. That wasn't going to buy the kind of horse I had pictured in my mind. Things looked depressingly hopeless. After pulling into town for the next rodeo, someone told me about a paint stallion a local family owned that was for sale. I drove out to their place and saw him. He was standing in a pen, in mud up to his knees and hocks. He was beautiful! I immediately felt he was my horse. I drove back to the rodeo grounds and tracked down his owner and asked about the horse. He began telling me how this horse had been shown in halter and had won the state title in Minnesota. My hopes in buying him were quickly circling the toilet. He said he was priced at $10k. Well, now my hopes weren't just circling the drain…they were flushed entirely. The man asked what I wanted to do with him, and I told him, but quickly and politely excused myself so as to go cry somewhere.

Isn't it something how a "sucky attitude" just seems to attract more "suckiness?" My miserable attitude had just descended to a brand-new low. The next night, I was to do the music for a Bible study held in someone's barn. Lo and behold, the man who owned the stallion came walking in along with his wife. He approached me and proceeded to give me a framed picture of the horse when he won the Minnesota title. He then began telling me that he had always felt this horse was destined for something special, and God had laid it on his and his wife's heart to give me the horse! I burst out in tears over this great sacrificial gift! God later spoke to me about how I could never out give Him. My former sucky attitude was instantly replaced with repentance and great thankfulness, along with renewed humility. If I'd gotten paid for every "perf" for the last several years, I couldn't have saved enough money to buy that horse. You simply can't outgive God!

Performing on Max at the PRCA Rodeo in Manawa, WI

Performing "Liberty" at Mid-West
Horse Fair, Madison, WI 2017

PERSEVERANCE

Before Tyger graduated high school, he started saying he wanted to be an army ranger. As with all of us at that age, his mettle had not yet been tested to that degree. But with all of us, sooner or later, as it pertains to destiny, our mettle WILL be tested. Sure enough, years later as a paratrooper in the 82nd, he finally got his chance to compete for an opening into ranger school. Five weeks of pre-ranger PT with a hundred guys trying out for only twelve openings, and Tyger landed a spot. He was ecstatic, as was I!

Ranger school has three phases: the Darby, Mountain, and Swamp. Each has its own incredible difficulties, but one thing runs through the entire process. It is literally controlled starvation and sleep deprivation for sixty-three days…IF a guy doesn't re-cycle and have to do a phase over again. To earn the coveted Ranger Tab, they must demand things from their body that are beyond what most are capable of doing so as to find those men with a strong enough will to keep pushing themselves when their body is literally screaming to quit.

Tyger re-cycled both the Darby and the Mountain Phases, making his time in ranger school two-hundred-plus days. We're talking almost an entire year of…as Tyger says…"a suck fest." At the end of all that time, he ended up NOT getting the Ranger Tab he had dreamed of for so many years, and worked so hard to attain. When he called to tell me, I cried. He did some crying too. It was heartbreaking. As we mothers do, I tried to console him by saying that though none of this made sense right now, it would later on. Although I believed what I said 100 percent, I knew it wouldn't make things easier to handle. Heartbreak is heartbreak…any way you slice it. You just gotta walk through that pain. Notice I said THROUGH. Heartbreak of any kind is not meant to be a destination, it's an event! It only becomes a destination if you quit moving forward and camp there.

I knew Tyger wouldn't settle for failure. *Tuff* IS his middle name. It took two full years for him to regain the confidence and the heart to be willing to face the "suck fest" again and give it another try. Another chance came, and a slot opened. This time he sailed through the sixty-three days without recycling any phase and got his well-earned Ranger Tab. He had discovered the reason he failed in his first attempt. His first time through, he was only thinking of passing the course for himself. His second time, he had the mindset to do all that was possible to help every man in his team pass the course. He got one of the highest peer ratings in that school because he was working above and beyond what was expected of him to help his team succeed.

He had matured. Where he failed the first time, it had taught him a hard lesson that later enabled him to succeed because he persevered. Quitting would have been SO EASY. I wish lessons could always be learned in a climate-controlled classroom, but that's simply not the case. Some of the best lessons we learn are learned, as they say, in the school of hard knocks. Tyger not only gained a Ranger Tab, he also gained a new level of integrity and maturity that remains a part of a person's character forever. There's just some things that you cannot attain without perseverance.

Broken Wood
by Tyger Tuff Lyons

The tall proud tree by axe unbroken
Stands high upon his hilltop perch
And by the light of morning woken
Scoffs at the ships below in berth

Flighty ships of broken wood
Who once were tall and proud as he
At once brought low from whence they stood
A tragic end for any tree

Yet flighty ships of broken wood
Which once as trees had grown
Had seen a world beyond the hill
The only hill that tree had known

They knew of waves and gales and reefs
Of fog's great fear and land ho's thrill
While the tall proud tree whose roots went deep
Stood motionless upon the hill

If not for cutting of strong trees
Would be no ships that stood
For in the breaking is remaking
Mighty ships from broken wood

Not all felled trees become as ships
And some that do will surely fail
But spared the pain of axe's hits
No tall proud tree would ever sail

Tyger was a hungry but HAPPY camper to finish ranger school and get his Ranger Tab!

Very FIRST item on the agenda after being released from sixty-three days of ranger school…EAT!

THE GLORIOUS ADVENTURE

I was sitting on the floor in front of the TV, minding my own business, watching the tenth go-round of the National Finals Rodeo, at that time being held in Oklahoma City, Oklahoma. I suddenly felt the presence of God settling down upon me, and His voice began to speak inside me. He said, "I'm going to take you to the NFR, and you will not be a ticket-paying spectator." I also heard the words "Las Vegas." First off, at that time, the NFR had ALWAYS been in Oklahoma City, and no one ever expected that to change. Secondly, I was only a goat tyer in the amateurs and only world-class barrel racers made it to the NFR. But it was so heavy upon me, I knew it was God speaking to me, and I simply believed Him.

Not long after that encounter, God began talking to me about rodeo being a "god" in my heart, and He was asking me to lay it down. Did I say asking? A more accurate statement would be nagging! It was an inward battle that simply would NOT leave me alone. I look back now and am amazed that such a little thing as goat tying in amateur rodeos meant so much to me! But as always…God was right. I was desperate for an identity other than the one I seemed to be stuck in. Living in the Ozarks of southern Missouri, I held an insatiable desire to be a cowgirl. Since I didn't possess a barrel horse, goat tying was my ONLY option. The nerve of God to ask…no, demand…that I give up the only thing I had that gave me an escape from the drudgery that seemed to be my "lot in life."

After several weeks of being miserable because of the unceasing war that was going on inside me, I gave it up. Grudgingly…VERY grudgingly. I'd like to say I yielded in joyful submission, but it was more like throwing my hands down, along with my sucker, in the dirt. But from that moment on, I never entered another rodeo for two full years. It was amazing to me, but I actually didn't miss it. God had done what I could never do; He took that desire out of my heart, and I was no longer its slave.

To keep this short story from becoming a novel, let me skip a lot of explanation and just say that after two years, the Lord spoke to me about entering a rodeo. But weirder than that, He was inviting me to enter an all-girl rodeo in Alma, Arkansas, in the bull riding! I had never been on a bull in my life. I was thirty years old at the time, and I was just supposed to go get on a bull?? That's crazy…even by my standards! After praying about what was going on inside me, I asked a bull rider friend of mine if he would go with me, allow me to use his equipment, and put me on a bull. His response was, "This sounds like fun!" (Cowboys…always enjoying the entertainment supplied by someone else's stupidity.)

That first bull may be the subject of another short story, but suffice it to say, twelve bulls later, I was in the running for Rookie of the Year in the Women's Professional Rodeo Association. One afternoon, I received a call that went something like this: "Pro Rodeo Stock Contractor, Jim Sutton has an idea to further promote the crowning of Miss Rodeo America at the NFR. He wants six past World Champion Cowgirls involved. Three to ride bulls and three to ride bareback broncs. Although you are not a world champion, we feel you are to be one of the six girls. We'll pay you $500 to come to Vegas and get on a bull at the NFR." Tears were literally streaming down my face as I listened, remembering the word of the Lord to me a few years back, that He would take me to the NFR in Las Vegas. That one phone call literally changed the course of my life.

I am convinced that if I would've held on to MY WILL and not laid down goat tying, God could never have given me HIS WILL—and that was far greater than anything I could've dreamed up! God has such good plans for each one of us, but if we fight to have our own way, we can unknowingly sabotage our future and forfeit the very fulfillment of our heart's desires!

A verse in Luke 2 speaking of Jesus's birth into the earth gives a simple yet profound clue to living life to the fullest. It says that Mary laid Jesus in a manger, BECAUSE…Stop right there. There was a REASON Jesus was manifested in such a humble, insignificant place among insignificant people. The REASON the King was manifested in a cave housing animals and laid in a feed trough instead of a cradle was because He ALWAYS comes where room has been made, no matter how humble. He was there, because there was no room made for Him in the inn, nor anywhere else. God will ALWAYS show up and manifest Himself where room is made for Him!

Unknowingly, when I obeyed God and laid down my desire for rodeo, I made room for Jesus to manifest Himself in my life. He then blew my expectations out of the water and gave me something that I could never have imagined in my wildest dreams! Obedience always makes room for Jesus to do the greater. What is it that the Lord is asking of you right now? What nagging thing is going on inside you that you don't want to face? Don't bow up and resist it, going your own way. Whenever Jesus asks for anything, it's never to TAKE…it's always for the purpose of MAKING ROOM for something far greater. It's the doorway into fulfilled desires. Go for it! Lay aside what you're holding on to with white knuckles, yield to HIS PLANS, and let your adventure begin!

Riding at the NFR during the crowning of Miss Rodeo America on an old NFR bull named Brown Out, 1986

WHAT ABOUT YOU?

Where do you stand with the Lord? If you don't know, you need to know...and you CAN know. That's part of the great news about the Creator...He's approachable. He WANTS to be known. Knowing someone in reality is more than "hearing about them." It takes EXPERIENCE. It's gotta be relational, or it's not worth salt. We all need to learn "about God," but that alone doesn't get you there. I can know "about" someone, but that doesn't necessarily give them the right to have any authority in my life, and it sure doesn't mean I can trust them. God wants to show Himself REAL in your life! YOU hold the keys to allowing or disallowing the Lord Jesus to enter into you...cleansing you of all sin...giving you fresh hope and renewing your life. It's a REAL EXPERIENCE...not simply a religious belief system! Invite Jesus to be LORD of your whole life! Just be real. Open up your heart to Him and invite Him in; ask Him to reveal Himself to you and begin the relationship you were born to have with the Creator. Let the great adventure begin!!

For the longing of my Father is that everyone who
embraces the Son and believes in Him will experience
eternal life and I will raise them up in the last day.

—John 6:40 (Passion Translation)